THE ARCHITECTURAL HISTORY OF

Canterbury Cathedral

Also available from Tiger of the Stripe

HENRY SWEET
The Student's Dictionary of Anglo-Saxon

THOMAS FROGNALL DIBDIN
The Bibliomania or Book-Madness

Forthcoming

THE VENERABLE BEDE
Ecclesiastical History of the English People

GEOFFREY OF MONMOUTH
History of the Kings of Britain

EDWARD MAUNDE THOMPSON
The History of English Handwriting
A.D. 700–1400

WALTER MAP
Courtiers' Trifles

THE ARCHITECTURAL HISTORY OF

Canterbury Cathedral

THE REV. R. WILLIS MA, FRS, &C.

Jacksonian Professor of the University of Cambridge

TIGER OF THE STRIPE · RICHMOND · MMVI

This edition first published 2006 by
TIGER OF THE STRIPE
50 Albert Road
Richmond
Surrey TW10 6DP
United Kingdom

ISBN 1 904799 04 3

Book originally published 1845

Also available as an eBook from
http://www.ebooks.com

Printed in the United Kingdom
and the United States of America by
Lightning Source

𝕮able of 𝕮ontents

Preface   vii
Publisher's Introduction   ix
Introduction   xiii

Chapter 1 The architectural history of Canterbury Cathedral,
    from the earliest period to the year 1130; translated from
    the works of Edmer the singer, and others   1
Chapter 2 On the plan and arrangement of the Saxon
    cathedral   23
Chapter 3 Here beginneth Gervase his history of the burning
    and repair of the church of Canterbury   35
Chapter 4 On the church of Lanfranc   71
Chapter 5 On the works of Ernulf and the two Williams   81
Chapter 6 The history of the choir from the twelfth
    century   109
Chapter 7 The history of the nave, tower, and western
    transepts, from the end of the twelfth century   133
Chapter 8 The monuments   145

List of the burial places of the Archbishops of
    Canterbury   150
Explanation of the plan and section   153
A list of the dated examples of architectural works in
    Canterbury Cathedral   154
List of the principal works and editions referred to   157
Additional notes, and corrections   159
Index   161

Preface

THE TRANSLATION OF GERVASE, which it is the principal object of the following history to illustrate, was read by me with a few necessary omissions at the evening meeting of the Architectural Section of the British Archæological Association, on the 11th of September 1844, and on the following morning I had the honor of explaining to a numerous audience in the cathedral itself, the application of this translation to the building, and also of pointing out those later parts of which the history has been recorded, and which are the subject of the concluding chapters. The work may therefore be considered as forming part of the Transactions of the Association in question, although it is obviously too bulky and independent for insertion in the Journal, which is the recognised organ of that body. In preparing it for the press, however, I have made many additions to it, including especially the entire history of the Saxon cathedral; and on a subsequent visit, with the able assistance of Mr. De la Motte, the drawings were made which illustrate its pages. These, however, have no pretensions to form a complete delineation of the building, architecturally speaking, which would plainly have required larger paper and a different material. And this delineation has been so well effected by previous publishers, especially in the work of Mr. Britton, to whose admirable plates I have referred throughout, that I had the less motive for attempting it. The sections of moldings which I have given were all, with the exception of a few that were inaccessible, drawn with the cymagraph, and reduced for the engraver by the help of the pantograph and camera lucida, their contours may therefore be depended upon for precision. The cloisters, chapter-house, and other monastic buildings connected with the cathedral, are of the most interesting character, but their history is so completely distinct, and would have extended this work so much beyond its proper limits, that I have reserved them entirely for the subject of a future essay.

Publisher's Introduction

A REPRINT OF ROBERT WILLIS'S CLASSIC TEXT on Christ Church of 1845 needs no apology, except, perhaps, to admit that it is one hundred and sixty years overdue. Not only does the scholarship stand up to modern scrutiny, but the superb wood engravings offer a clarity which is hard to achieve with the best modern photography.

The author's technique was to read the documentary evidence and relate it to his own observations of the cathedral's surviving structure. In principle, nothing could be simpler, but in practice it requires an exceptional grasp of medieval Latin, an understanding of both architecture and liturgy, and a most perceptive eye.

Robert Willis

It is hard to imagine a modern architectural history of Canterbury Cathedral being written by the inventor of a patented pedal harp and a machine for designing gearwheels, a man who had a special interest in speech synthesis, whose lectures on applied mechanics were enjoyed by many. Nonetheless, these were among Willis's many achievements.

Robert Willis (1800–1875) graduated BA from Gonville and Caius College, Cambridge, in 1826 as ninth wrangler. He won both the Schuldham Plate, awarded to the leading graduand chosen from all subjects, and a Frankland Fellowship. He went on to be Jacksonian Professor of natural and experimental philosophy at Cambridge in 1837, and from 1854 combined this with a lectureship in applied mechanics at the Metropolitan School of Science in Jermyn Street, London. Here he, T. H. Huxley and others gave a biennial course of lectures for working men, to which Karl Marx subscribed.

His inventions included the tabuloscriptive engine for making numeric tables into graphs (a sort of mechanical Excel charting device) and the odontograph for laying out the teeth of gearwheels. As he indicates in his Preface (p. vii), he used various mechanical devices to aid in recording the architecture of Canterbury Cathedral, including a camera lucida, cymagraph[1] and pantograph. Although he was a skilled draftsman himself, he also benefited from the services of one of the talented Delamotte family of artists, probably Freeman Gage Delamotte (c. 1813–1862).

Editorial Policy

I had originally intended to produce a simple facsimile of the original edition, but the poor state of my copy, with serious foxing on some pages, made this almost impossible. Once launched upon resetting the text, it seemed to be sensible to make some corrections and amendments. Nonetheless, I was unwilling to make any major changes to what is a classic.

It has not been possible, or even desirable, to maintain the original pagination. This has the disadvantage that it is difficult to relate a page reference to the new. The advantage is that (with the exception of Figs 3/4 and 5/6, each pair of which is drawn together in reverse order) the illustrations now appear in the correct order. It should also be noted that Fig. 24, a view in the north aisle, looking north-west, is still missing, as it was in 1845!

The original footnote labelling has been retained, with all its quirks – as a medievalist, Willis does not usually distinguish between *i* and *j* or *u*, *v* and *w*, so *k* follows *i* and *x* follows *u*, but he has notes *j* on pp. 41, 59 and 109, and a note *v* on p. 46. There are two footnotes *e* in a row, on pp. 127 and 129.

---

1 Willis described the cymagraph to the Institute of British Architects on 27 February 1837 as 'a new instrument invented by him for tracing profiles and mouldings', *Athenæum*, 11 March 1837, p. 179.

Willis's spelling has been retained in most instances, including *mold/molding* rather than *mould/moulding*, although *quire* (a spelling which on etymological grounds should be relegated to the meaning of four sheets folded together to create an eight-leaf gathering) and *cript* seemed rather extreme and have been corrected, except in quoting third parties. Even proper names have usually been left unchanged, so *Ælfheah* is referred to as *Elfege* or *Elphege* and *Eadwine* as *Edwyn*. A few of the more common names, such as *William of Malmesbury* have been changed to their more familiar forms.

Literals, such as *sinepealt* for *sinewealt* (p. 42, where the typesetter confused wyn and thorn in the Old English fount) have also been corrected.

Single rather than double quotation marks have been used in conformity with modern UK book publishing practice. Other punctuation and capitalisation has been adjusted for clarity. I have italicised the titles of printed books and journals but have left unpublished works in Roman type. Of course, most of Willis's references are of limited use today, so I have listed some more recent ones in the following section.

Except for a little resizing and touching up, illustrations are unchanged. Unfortunately, there is little chance that modern digital techniques will be able to match the superb quality of the original wood engravings.

Some Modern Editions of Sources Referred to by Willis

Bede, *Ecclesiastical History of the English People*, Leo Sherley-Price trans., D. H. Farmer ed., rev. edn, Penguin, 1990.

Eadmer of Canterbury, *Eadmer's History of recent events in England: Historia novorum in Anglia*, Geoffrey Bosanquet trans., Cresset Press, 1964.

Eadmer of Canterbury, *The life of St Anselm, Archbishop of Canterbury*, R. W. Southern ed. and trans., rev. edn, Clarendon Press, 1972.

Eadmer of Canterbury, *Lives and Miracles of Saints Oda, Dunstan, and Oswald,* Bernard J. Muir and Andrew J. Turner eds, Oxford University Press, 2006.

Lanfranc, *The Monastic Constitutions of Lanfranc,* David Knowles ed. and trans., Christopher N. L. Brooke rev., rev. edn, Clarendon Press, 2002.

John Leland, *John Leland's Itinerary: Travels in Tudor England,* John Chandler ed., Sutton Publishing, 1998

William of Malmesbury, *The Deeds of the Bishops of England (Gesta Pontificum Anglorum),* Boydell Press, 2002.

William of Malmesbury, *Gesta Pontificum Anglorum, The History of the English Bishops,* vol. 1, Michael Winterbottom and Rodney Malcolm Thomson eds, Oxford University Press, due to be published 2007.

Further Reading

For those with a reasonable grasp of Latin, the Rolls Series published in the nineteenth century by Her Majesty's Stationery Office provide a very wide range of source materials. These books are available in most humanities collections.

Recent archæology has tended to confirm the reliability of Eadmer, Willis's source for the Anglo-Saxon church. All readers, with or without an archæological background, will find much absorbing information in the works of the Canterbury Archæological Trust. In particular, they are recommended to read:

Kevin Blockley, Margaret Sparks and Tim Tatton-Brown eds, *Canterbury Cathedral Nave: Archæology, History and Architecture,* The Archæology of Canterbury New Series, vol. 1, Dean & Chapter of Canterbury Cathedral and Canterbury Archæological Trust, 1997.

PETER DANCKWERTS
Richmond, May 2006

Introduction

THE CATHEDRAL WHICH IS THE SUBJECT of the following pages is remarkable for its extent, beauty, and importance, for the variety of its architectural styles, for the changes of plan and structure which it has undergone, and especially for the numerous historical particulars relating to these changes which have been preserved to us.

By a careful investigation of the architectural history of Canterbury cathedral, we may therefore expect to obtain great insight into the motives that dictated such changes of plan and structure in all similar buildings, as well as a knowledge of the mode of their erection, and of the causes that led to those well known varieties of style that form so interesting and at the same time so perplexing a subject for investigation.

Amongst the other difficulties of such enquiries, two are prominent: first, that of understanding the exact meaning of the historical documents, which is too often obscured by our imperfect knowledge of their technical terms; next, the uncertainty which often occurs with respect to the application of the documents to the buildings that exist.

I have endeavoured, therefore, throughout this history, to separate as much as possible my own opinions and interpretations from the historical documents upon which they are based. It will be found that I have given in each case the written records in their own words as closely as translation would allow, and usually accompanied in the notes by the passages in the original language. I have done this partly because the words and phrases and sentiments of a coeval writer appear to me to possess an interest so great, that every change, every attempt to modernize them, must deteriorate from their value, and from the pleasure and instruction which they convey to their readers. Partly also because the rapid strides which are now making in architectural history, may probably weaken or correct many of my interpretations; and by thus separating the evidence from the opinions, the foundation of each will always be manifest and the correction rendered more easy, while the history, as a collection of evidence, will lose none of its value. My plan therefore has been, first to collect all the written evidence, and then by a close comparison of it with the building itself, to make the best identification of one with the other that I have been able.

I have also confined myself strictly to the history of the building, without mixing up with it the history of the see, which most writers upon this subject have been tempted to do. Thus the mission of Augustine, vast and important as its consequences were, has for my purpose no other result worth noting than the recovery of the ancient Christian church at Canterbury, the work of the Roman believers, which in the course of ages grew up into the huge fabric of the present cathedral; and the murder of Thomas à Becket only concerns me as the cause of the removal of the pillar and vault which originally occupied the scene of his death, and as the motive which led to the erection of the magnificent eastern termination of the cathedral; and perhaps as the source of the wealth which enabled the monks to re-erect the church on so extensive a plan. On the other hand, various events so trifling, that they would be neglected altogether in a history of the see, require in a history of the building a complete and prominent notice if they even affect the change of position of a door or the reconstruction of a window.

It is impossible to understand the intricacies and changes of these buildings unless we take the trouble to examine the purposes for which they were constructed, and steadily recollect the state of learning and religious opinions at the same period. A vision, or the supposed acquisition of the relics of some noted saint, were often reasons which led to the erection or enlargement of a considerable church or chapel, the plan of which is usually distributed so as to display these latter treasures to the greatest advantage.

In the following history I have shewn how the gradual acquirement of relics, and the accumulation of sainted archbishops, led from one addition to another to the present complicated plan of the structure. The language in which the history is clothed by the original writers will shew that they considered a provision for the repose of the saints to be one of the principal objects for which the building was erected. This may serve as my apology for having so often quoted passages which relate to the relics and entombment of the saints and archbishops.

I have been the more tempted to do this, because the minute descriptions of such objects by Gervase (whose tract on the cathedral I have given entire) enables us to assign the local position of most of them; and I have been desirous of presenting to my readers a picture of the manner in which these buildings were in the old time occupied in all directions by shrines, altars, and monuments, and obstructed by screens and lofts, roods and reredoses, in singular contrast to the modern attempts to throw open and expose to sight as much as can be by any possibility seen at one view. This at any rate is in flat opposition to the intention of the original contrivers of such structures.

I must also plead guilty to the introduction of certain miraculous narratives in the earlier part of the history. It will be found, however, that each legend contains some indirect evidence relating to the arrangement or construction of the building, which is wholly independent of the miraculous part of the story. And as the narrators are usually speaking of buildings with which themselves and their readers at that time were well acquainted, we may be quite sure that what they say of the building is true, however they may deceive themselves and others with respect to the supernatural interpretations which the habits of thought in those days led them to give to the events in question.

The most remarkable medieval writer of architectural history is undoubtedly Gervase. Himself a monk of Christ Church at the time of Becket's death, and an eye-witness of the fire in 1174, and of the rebuilding of the church, he has left us a most valuable and minute account of the latter events in his tract 'On the burning and repair of the Church of Canterbury.' The information thus conveyed is not confined to the church in question, but gives us a general insight into the modes of proceeding in the carrying on of buildings at that period, the manner of providing architects, the time consumed in erecting these structures, the way in which old portions were adopted and worked up, the temporary expedients for carrying on the daily service, the care which was taken of the venerated remains unavoidably disturbed by the progress of the work, and many other most instructive particulars which occur in every page of this circumstantial writer. For these reasons it has always appeared to me that a complete translation of his book would supply an exceedingly useful help to architectural investigation. It is true that the complete original was most excellently printed in the well known collection of Chronicles, usually called the 'Decem Scriptores,' and that considerable extracts from it have been translated by every subsequent writer on Canterbury cathedral. But the work loses its interest by being served up piecemeal, and I have therefore given it entire in a new translation,[a] and have endeavoured to supply a more close and particular comparison of the text with the existing building than has been hitherto undertaken. A task the more easy from the consistency and evident veracity of our historian in the most minute particulars.

But Gervase confines his history to the few years of his own experience, first describing the church as he knew it before the fire, then the events of the fire, and lastly the progress of the rebuilding. The previous and subsequent history of the structure must be

---

[a] I have not given the original Latin text of Gervase, because it would have swelled the book unnecessarily, and is printed entire in a work of easy reference. The case is very different from the detached quotations with which these pages are filled, for the original Latin below saves the trouble of searching through a number of books and particular editions of books which may not be accessible to every reader.

supplied from other sources. The most copious authority for the early history is Edmer (or Eadmer) the singer, that is, the cantor or precentor of the cathedral. He was a boy in the school of the monastery when Lanfranc began to pull down the Saxon cathedral in order to erect his own, and he also lived under the rule of Anselm and his successor Radulph. He wrote a history of his own times, and a volume of Opuscula, consisting principally of biographies of the archbishops. From these works may be gathered a number of particulars of the Saxon cathedral and of the Norman one which succeeded. These of course have not the value of a continuous narrative like that of Gervase, because we can never be certain that some important link in the chain of events may not be wanting, because it did not happen to be connected with the person whose life was the immediate object of the writer we are quoting. But this is unfortunately the case with the greater part of structural history. Few medieval writers made a building the theme of their literary efforts, and even Gervase thinks it necessary to apologize for writing about the mere putting together of stones, by explaining his object to be the description of the resting-places of the saints. The monastic writers usually enumerate the building or repairing of a church, or part of it, amongst the good works of their ecclesiastics, and from such disjointed hints, for the most part, we must be content to heap together our architectural histories. Thus from Edmer and a few other authorities I have compiled the first chapter, mostly from well known materials, which I have tried to give as nearly as possible in the words of the originals, leaving my own comments and interpretations of their meaning to the subsequent chapters. But I can lay no claim to literary research in the following pages. Everyone who is acquainted with the writings of Somner, Battely, Dart, Gostling, Wharton, &c., must know that every available source of information has been already indicated, and indeed for the most part printed by them.

All that is left for their successors is the far easier task of the selection and classification of their materials, and the application of them to the buildings in existence. This application must of course be made by each new writer after his own fashion. I have endeavoured to make a closer comparison step by step between the documents and the masonry than has yet been attempted; with what success my readers must judge. But I cannot conclude without expressing my most grateful thanks to the Dean and Chapter of the cathedral, and to their architect, Mr. Austin, for the most liberal and unbounded freedom of access to every part of the building, accompanied by every kind of assistance and information; without which it would have been impossible for me to have carried on my researches.

Chapter 1

THE ARCHITECTURAL HISTORY OF CANTERBURY CATHEDRAL, FROM THE EARLIEST PERIOD TO THE YEAR 1130; TRANSLATED FROM THE WORKS OF EDMER THE SINGER, AND OTHERS

IN THIS CHAPTER I propose to relate the history of the building. and the events which bore upon its construction, arrangement, and changes, and to do this in the words of the original authors as much as possible. To this effect I have divided it into distinct and numbered articles. Each of these is translated from the corresponding passage quoted at the foot of the page unless the contrary is stated, for in some cases I have found it necessary to give an abstract only of some events that affected the building, and yet did not require to be related at length; such as the sack of Canterbury by the Danes. As this chapter is pieced together from various works, I have usually given the original Latin below, omitting it only when a long narrative has been abridged from the Anglia Sacra, or some other book of common occurrence. I have added dates, and numbered each archbishop in the order of his succession.

1

A.D. 602

*"When Augustine (the first archbishop of Canterbury) assumed the episcopal throne in that royal city, he recovered therein, by the king's assistance, a church which, as he was told, had been constructed by the original labour of Roman believers. This church he consecrated in the name of the Saviour, our God and Lord Jesus Christ; and there he established an habitation for himself, and for all his successors.

---

a 'At Augustinus, ubi in regia civitate sedem episcopalem, ut prædiximus, accepit; recuperavit in ea, regio fultus adminiculo, ecclesiam, quam inibi antiquo Romanorum fidelium opere factam fuisse didicerat, et eam in nomine sancti Salvatoris Dei et Domini nostri Jesu Christi sacravit, atque ibidem sibi habitationem statuit et cunctis successoribus suis.' Bedæ, *Ecc. Hist.* 1. i. c. 33.

2

A.D. 740
to 758

Cuthbert[b] (the eleventh archbishop), amongst his other good works, constructed a church to the east of the great church, and almost touching it, which he solemnly dedicated in honour of St. John the Baptist. He fabricated this church for the following purposes; that baptisms might be celebrated therein; that certain judicial trials, which are wont to be held in the church, might be carried on there; and lastly, that the bodies of the archbishops might therein be buried; thus departing from the ordinary ancient custom of burial beyond the walls of the city. And he was accordingly buried in the aforesaid church of St. John.

3

A.D. 740

'For when Cuthbert went to Rome to receive the pallium from Pope Gregory, he obtained from him, that all future archbishops might be buried in the church of Canterbury, and that a cemetery should be made within that city. From the earliest times, the kings of Kent, the archbishops, and the monks of Christ Church, as well as the people of the city, had been buried in the atrium or churchyard of the church of the Apostles Peter and Paul, beyond the walls. For the Romans, who were first sent into England, said that the city was for the living, and not for the dead. But now by Divine permission, and at the request of Cuthbert, it was ordained by Pope Gregory, with the consent of King Eadbrith, that the archbishops of Canterbury should be buried in their own church, to the intent that they might have their resting-place where they had living ruled in honour.[d]

---

b 'Is inter alia bona… fecit Ecclesiam in orientali parte majoris Ecclesiæ eidem penè contiguam; eamque in honorem beati Johannis Baptistæ solenniter dedicavit, &c…' Edmer. Vito S. Bregwini, *Ang. Sac.,* t. ii. p. 186. See also Osbern. in *Ang. Sac.,* t. ii. p. 75.

c A literal translation from Gervase, Act. Pont. Cant., p. 1640.

d Of the successors of Outhbert, it is recorded that Bregwin (the twelfth) and Athelard (the fourteenth) were buried in St. John's church. Jambert (the thirteenth) having been abbot of St. Augustine, chose to be buried there; and after Athelard, the archbishops are said to have been buried in Christ Church: but perhaps this term includes the church of St. John. Vide *Ang. Sac.,* t. i. p. 85. Gervase, pp. 1295 and 1641.

4   [e]Archbishop Bregwin (the twelfth) was buried in the afore-
A.D. 762   said church of St. John, near the body of the reverend Cuthbert. His tomb was flat, of decent workmanship, and a little
raised above the pavement.

5   [f]Archbishop Plegemund (the nineteenth) journeyed to
Rome, and bought the blessed martyr Blasius for a great
A.D.891   sum of gold and silver. He brought the body with him when
he returned to Canterbury, and placed it there in Chriſt Church.

6   [g]In the days of Archbishop Odo (the twenty-second) the
roof of Chriſt Church had become rotten from excessive
A.D. 940
to 960   age, and reſted throughout upon half-shattered pieces:
wherefore he set about to reconſtruct it, and being also desirous of
giving to the walls a more aſpiring altitude, he directed his assembled workmen to remove altogether the disjointed ſtructure above,

e Edmer, Vit. Bregw. *Ang. Sac.*, t. ii. p. 187. and MS. C.C.C. p. 286. '... Planum si-
quidem sepulchrum fuit, paulum a pavimento decenti opere altius ſtructum.' (Also
Osbern. p. 76.)

f 'Plegemundus archiepiscopus Romam profectus eſt, et beatum martyrem Blasium
cum multa pecunia auri et argenti emit et secum rediens Cantuariam detulit et in ecclesia Chriſti collocavit.' Gerv. Act. Pont. Cant. p. 1644.

g 'Tectum ejusdem Ecclesiæ Chriſti nimiâ vetuſtate corruptum, semirutis per totum
partibus pendebat. Quod ille renovare cupiens, murum quoque in porrectiorem celsi-
tudinem exaltari desiderans, congregatis artificibus præcepit et quod dissolutum desuper eminebat penitus tolli, et quod minus in altitudine murus habebat jussit extolli.
Sed quia clerus ac populus absque divino servitio esse non valebat; et tantæ magnitudi-
nis templum non reperiebatur, quæ ad capiendam numerosæ plebis multitudinem
sufficere videretur; deprecatus eſt Pontifex Dominum ut quousque opus incæptum
consummatum fuisset, nulla aut infusio imbrium aut vis ventorum infra parietes Ecclesiæ descenderet quæ eos à divino opere prohibere valerent. Factumque eſt; ut in
tribus annis quibus Ecclesiæ muri in altum porrigebantur, tota fabrica desuper pa-
teret, nec tamen non dico infra ambitum solius Ecclesiæ, sed nec intra muros totius
civitatis imber aliquando descenderet, qui vel clerum in Ecclesiâ Chriſti consiſtentem
ab officio præpediret, vel populum ad Ecclesiam concurrentem aliquatenus posset ab
incæpto cohibere. Eratque res digna ſpectaculo; cum videres omnia civitatis pomæria
aquis infundi, et ejus mœnia nulla pluviarum inundatione madefieri.' Edmer. Vit.
Odonis, *Ang. Sac.*, t. ii. p. 83.

The same ſtory is told in other words by the same author, in his Life of S. Oswald...
'parietes Ecclesiæ Chriſti Dorobernensis... in altiorem quam erat ſtatum sublato tecto
ipse pater conſtruere volens, &c... ' (*Ang. Sac.*, p. 193). Also by Malmesbury.

and commanded them to supply the deficient height of the walls by raising them. But because it was absolutely necessary that the Divine Service should not be interrupted, and no temple could be found sufficiently capacious to receive the multitude of the people, the archbishop prayed to Heaven that until the work should be completed, neither rain nor wind might be suffered to intrude within the walls of the church, so as to prevent the performance of the service. And so it came to pass: for during three years in which the walls of the church were being carried upwards, the whole building remained open to the sky: yet did no rain fall either within the walls of the church, or even within the walls of the city, that could impede the clergy standing in the church in the performance of their duty, or restrain the people from coming even to the beginning of it. And truly it was a sight worth seeing, to behold the space beyond the walls of the city drenched with water, while the walls themselves remained perfectly dry.

7   [h]During the primacy of this good and holy Odo, it happened that in the course of one of his visitations he came to the monastery of Ripon, which had been founded by Wilfrid, and in the church of which his remains had been deposited. But at this time the place was reduced by wars and hostile incursions to a deserted and ruined solitude. Wherefore having opened the ground where the blessed Wilfrid was deposited, he reverently raised his bones and dust, with the intention of conveying them to his church at Canterbury. 'Nevertheless, lest the place which Wilfrid had loved above all others while he remained in the flesh, should be utterly deprived of all relies of him, he deposited there in a convenient place a small portion of them, and then, enriched with so great a treas-

---

h This article is abridged from a passage in Eadmer's Life of Wilfrid, which concludes with the following words: '… venerabilis Odo tanto munere locupletatus Cantuariam rediit ubi magna totius civitatis exsultatione susceptus et in aulam Dei sacra cum laude perductus, sanctissimas beati Wilfridi reliquias quas advexerat, in majori altare, quod in honorem Jesu Christi Domini nostri sacratum erat, collocavit…' Edm. Vito S. Wilfridi, Mabillon, t. iii p. 227. MS. C.C.C. p. 77.

ure, returned to Canterbury, where he was received by the whole population with great rejoicing, and accompanied to the house of God with solemn praises. He there placed the relics of the blessed Wilfrid which he had brought with him in the great Altar, which was consecrated in honour of our Lord Jesus Christ.'

8 It has been related to me by certain of the seniors of the convent, that in the time of King Edgar,[i] there came to England four clerks, who presented themselves at his court, and asserted that they had brought with them the body of Saint Audoen. And when the king refused to believe this, they appealed to the miraculous power which the relics possessed. Whereupon the king, thinking this to be a matter rather for ecclesiastical judgment than for his own, commanded the attendance of Archbishop Odo. And when he had succeeded in performing several miraculous cures by the contact of the relics in question, the truth of the story was no longer doubted; the king munificently rewarded the bearers of this treasure, and committed it to the charge of the archbishop, that it might be conveyed to Canterbury, and worthily deposited in Christ Church. As to the four clerks, they accompanied it thither, and were so well pleased with the monastery, that they became monks, and ended their days therein.[k]

---

[i] Edgar began his reign A.D. 957, about three years before the death of Odo; the year of Odo's death is however uncertain.

[k] Abridged from a diffuse narrative among the Opuscula of Edmer, bearing the following title: 'De reliquiis Sancti Audoeni, et quorundam aliorum sanctorum quæ Cantuariæ in Ecclesiæ domini Salvatoris habentur.' MS. C.C.C. p. 441. Audoen, otherwise called *Ouen* and *Dado*, was archbishop of Rouen, and died A.D. 686.

Capgrave has introduced the above legend into his Life of St. Audoen, in Edmer's words, but with some abridgments. It seems that another entire body of St. Audoen was preserved at Rouen, and detached relics of him elsewhere; which unlucky facts are the subject of grave discussion in the *Acta Sanctorum*. (August. t. iv. p. 803.) My purpose in introducing this and similar anecdotes, is merely to shew the successive acquisition of relics at Canterbury, which were then and there believed to be genuine, and which, together with the gradual accumulation of sainted archbishops, necessitated the plan, and successive enlargements of the present magnificent church.

9 [1]When the sacred bones of the blessed Father Audoen were brought to Canterbury, a precious and handsome coffer (scrinium) was made for them, according to the fashion of those days, in which they were decently laid, and carefully enwrapped in several winding-sheets. This took place about the same time that the venerable Odo had translated the body of the blessed Wilfrid, archbishop of York, from Ripon to Canterbury (as above related).

10 [m]Now on the day of the coming of Dunstan, the successor of Odo, to Canterbury, he was celebrating mass at the Altar A.D. 962 of the Saviour, when suddenly the house was covered with a cloud, and that dove which erst was seen of John in Jordan, again appeared, and hovered over him. And when the saerifice was completed, it rested upon the tomb of the blessed Odo, which was constructed in the fashion of a pyramid, to the south of the Altar.

11 Archbishop Dunstan (the twenty-fourth) was buried in the spot which he himself had chosen (two days before his A.D. 988 death), the place, to wit, where the Divine office was daily celebrated by the brethren, and which was before the steps which led up to the Altar of the Lord Christ. Here in the midst of the choir his body was deposited in a leaden coffin, deep in the ground, according to the ancient custom of the English, and the depth of his

---

l 'Igitur ubi sacratissima ossa beatissimi patris Audoeni Cantuariam delata sunt: scrinium illis pro illorum dierum qualitate factum est preciosum atque honestum in quo decenter diversis involumentis* obvoluta diligentissime collocata sunt. Ipsis pene diebus idem venerabilis Odo corpus beati Wilfridi pontificis Eboracensium de Rhipis sublatum Cantuariam transtulerat, &c...' (vide infra, Art. 15.) Edm. de Reliq. MS. C.C.C. p. 444.

m 'Cùm die adventus sui primò sacris altaribus assisteret[†]... repente contecta nube domo columba in Jordane à Johanne olim visa iterum apparuit; quæ quousque sacrificium fnisset consumptum, super illum mansit. Oumque consumptum fuisset sacrificium ; requievit supra memoriam Beati Odonis, quæ ad australem partem altaris in modum pyramidis exstructa fuit.' Osbernus de Vito Dunst., Ang. Sac., t. ii. p. 110.

* Involumen. *Linteum vero quo corpus involvitur, vulgo* Linceul, drap. (Du Cange).
† 'Ad Altare Domini Salvatoris Cantuariræ.' Edm. Vito Odonis. Ang. Sac. t. ii. p. 86.

grave was made equal to the stature of an ordinary man. A tomb was afterwards constructed over him, in the form of a large and lofty pyramid, and having at the head of the saint the matutinal Altar. Thus by choosing so conspicuous a spot, he left a mournful and tender memorial of himself to the brethren singing in the choir, or ascending the steps of the Altar.

12 In the primacy of Archbishop Elphege (the twenty-eighth) the sack of Canterbury by the Danes took place. During the A.D. 1011 massacre of the inhabitants, the monks barricaded themselves in the church. The archbishop at length rushed out, and appealed in vain to the conquerors, in favour of the people: he was immediately seized, and dragged back to the churchyard. 'Here these children of Satan piled barrels one upon another, and set them on fire, designing thus to burn the roof. Already the heat of the flames began to melt the lead, which ran down inside, when the monks came forth,'*o* and submitted to their fate: four only of their number escaped slaughter. 'And now that the people were slain, the city

---

n The passages whence the above article has been compiled are the following: '… Cum fratribus Ecclesiam Christi ingreditur, signatoque sepulchri sui loco omnibus ad Altare Christi ascendentibus conspicuo…' Osbern. Vito S. Dunst. Ang. Sac. t. ii. p. 117. 'Sepultus sane est in loco quo ipse disposuerat, loco scilicet ubi cotidie divinum officium a fratribus celebrabatur, quod fuit ante gradus quibus ad altare domini Christi ascendebatur.' Edm. Vito S. Dunstani, MS. C.C.C. p. 153. 'In medio chori ante gradus quibus ad majus Altare ascendebatur corpus Beati Dunstani humatum fuit in plumbeo loculo et illo in magna profunditate terrræ locato uti Anglis olim moris erat suorum cadavera tumulare.' Edm. Epistola. MS. C.C.C. 15. Ang. Sac. t. ii. p. 225. 'Infra terram ad staturam virilis corporis foveæ profunditas penetravit.' d°. d°… p. 224. 'Tumba super eum in modum pyramidis grandi sublimique constructa habente ad caput Sancti altare matutinale.' Edm. de Reliquiis. MS. C.C.C. p. 444. (vide infra. Art. 15.) 'In loco quem ante biduum ipse dictaverat cum diligentiâ sepultus et post hæc eminentioris operis structura decenter opertus, flebilem simul et amabilem cunctis sive in choro psallentibus seu per gradus ad Altare ascendentibus sui memoriam dereliquit.' Osbern. Vito S. Dunst., *Ang. Sac.,* t. ii. p. 119.

o 'Accedunt itaque filii Diaboli ad templum filii omnipotentis Dei; cuppas super invicem positas inflammant; tectum exinde molientes amburere. Jam plumbi materies à facie ignis resolutam cæpit introrsum defluere; cùm beata Monachorum plebs… egrediebatur, &c…'

burnt, and the church profaned, searched and despoiled;'[p] the arch-bishop was led away bound, and after enduring imprisonment and torture for seven months, was finally slain. His body was ransomed by the Londoners, and deposited with all reverence in their church of St. Paul. After ten or eleven years, we find the Christian Canute established on the throne, who repaired the monasteries which had been defiled and ruined in his own and his father's incursions,[q] and amongst various other acts by which his zeal for the Church was shewn, commanded the body of Elphege to be restored to his own church of Canterbury. Accordingly the body was raised, and conveyed thither from London with all possible so-lemnity and reverence, the king himself and Archbishop Egelnoth accompanying it to Christ Church, where it was deposited'.[r] The day of this translation (June 8th) was ever after observed at Canterbury.

A.D. 1023

p 'Jam populo cæso, jam urbe flammatâ, jam denique Christi templo violato, per-scrutato, spoliato, &c...' Osbern. Vito S. Elphegi, Ang. Sac. t. ii. p. 136.

q 'Monasteria per Angliam suis et patris excursionibus partim fœdata, partim eruta reparavit.' Will. Malm. 1. ii. c. 11.

r The events which occupy the above article, are related at great length by Osbern in his Life of Elphege, and in his account of the translation of his body. (Ang. Sac. t. ii.) As they exercised a direct influence upon the building, I found it necessary to give a short abstract of them, although they may be fouud in every history of England. In this I haye carefully presened the exact words of the original in the sentences that be-long expressly to the Church. For our present purpose it is only necessary to ascertain the exact amount of the damage. Now Gervase reckons this event as one of the fires that the cathedral suffered; namely, the first of the three. (Gerv., de Comb. p. 1291, and below.) And again in his Acts of the archbishops, he says the church was burnt and spoiled, 'Ecclesia Christi spoliata comburitur' (p. 1649). Edmer describing this event in the Historia Novorum asserts the same, 'Ecclesiam quoque Salvatoris flamma con sumpsit.' On the other hand, the same author in our next article will be found en-deavouring to explain that the flames neither destroyed the roof nor the walls, and it must be confessed, that the circumstantial narrative of Osbern, from which I have just given the exact words that apply to this matter, completely confirms Edmer's view, although a general historian might, in condensing the narrative, easily exaggerate the amount of the mischief done by the fire. No doubt Edmer is endeavouring in this last passage to represent the mischief to have been as small as possible; but whatever it might have been, it was evidently reparable without requiring any works of sufficient extent to alter or affect the arrangements or style of the building, for these repairs are scarcely noticed. We are left to infer that this church is to be included amongst those which Canute restored.

This 'Archbishop Egelnoth restored the Church of Canterbury to its former dignity.'[s] And King Canute gave to Christ Church his crown of gold, which is still kept at the head of the great cross, in the nave of the same.[t]

13 "It must be remarked, however, that the church itself at the time of the suffering of the blessed martyr Elphege, was neither consumed by the fire, nor were its walls or its roof destroyed. We know indeed that it was profaned and despoiled of many of its ornaments, and that the furious band attacked it, and applied fire from without to drive out the pontiff who was defending himself inside. But when they had laid hands upon him on his coming forth, they abandoned their fire, and other evil deeds which were addressed to his capture, and after slaying his monks before his eyes, they carried him away.

14 [x]After these things, and while misfortunes fell thick upon all parts of England, it happened that the city of Canterbury A.D. 1011 was set on fire by the carelessness of some individuals, and

---

s 'Cantuariensem Ecclesiam in statum pristinæ dignitatis reparavit,' &c. Gerv. Act. Pont. Cant. p. 1651. It does not follow however that this alludes to the building; more probably (from the context) to the influence and importance of the see.

t 'A.D. Mxxiij. Kanutus Rex dedit Ecclesiæ Christi in Dorobernia portum de Sandwico cum corona sua aurea quæ adhuc servatur in capite crucis majoris in navi ejusdem Ecclesiæ.' (Donationes, &c. Somner. App. p. 39). With respect to Sandwich, it must be remembered, that it forms no part of my plan to record this class of endowments.

About this time the province of Apulia was afflicted by a grievous famine; wherefore the bishop of Beneventum, being desirous of raising a sum of money to alleviate the sufferings of his people, travelled over Italy and France collecting gifts. He brought with him the arm-bone of St. Bartholomew, which he had abstracted from the body, and hearing of the great riches of England, he came hither, and in addition to the presents which he received, he sold the bone to Queen Emma for a large sum, and she presented it to the church of Canterbury. (Edm. Hist. Nov. p. 50.)

u 'Ecclesia ipsa in passione beatissimi martyris Elphegi nec igne consumpta nec tecto aut parietibus diruta fuit. Violatam quippe fuisse et pluribus ornamentis spoliatam, ac supposito de foris igne ut concremaretur adorsam novimus, quo vesana manus Pontificem intus sese tuentem quem mandaret exire compelleret. At ubi ipsum exeuntem comprehenderunt; omissis ignibus et aliis malis, quibus ad captionem illius occupabantur, ipsum necatis aliquibus monachis in oculis ejus abduxerunt.' Edm. Epist. de Corp. S. Dunst., Ang. Sac., t. ii. p. 225.

x This article is literally translated from Edmer (Vit. Bregwini, Ang. Sac., t. ii. p. 187).

that the rising flames caught the mother church thereof. How can I tell it?—the whole was consumed, and nearly all the monastic offices that appertained to it, as well as the church of the blessed John the Baptist, where as aforesaid the remains of the archbishops were buried. The exact nature and amount of the damage occasioned by that conflagration no man can tell. But its extent may be estimated, from the fact that the devouring flames consumed nearly all that was there preserved most precious, whether in ornaments of gold, of silver, or of other materials, or in sacred and profane books. Those things that could be replaced, were therefore the less to be regretted; but a mighty and interminable grief oppressed this Church because the privileges granted by the popes of Rome, and by the kings and princes of this kingdom, all carefully sealed and colleeted together, by which they and theirs were bound to defend and uphold the Church for ever, were now reduced to ashes. Copies of these documents were sought for, and collected from every place where such things were preserved : but their bulls and seals were irrecoverably destroyed with the church in which they had been deposited.

15 This was that very church (asking patience for a digression) which had been built by ᶨRomans, as Bede bears witness in his history, and which was duly arranged in some parts in

---

ᶨ The description which occupies this article, is quoted by Gervase in the tract 'de combustione' of which a translation will be found in the third chapter of this work, and of which the original text is ably edited in the *Decem Scriptores*. As far as I know, the source from whence Gervase obtained this passage, has been hitherto considered to have been lost, although he plainly refers to 'Edmerus venerabilis cantor in opusculis suis,' and a collection of the works of Edmer are preserved in the library of Corpus Christi Coll. under the very title 'Opuscula Edmeri Cantoris,' which although not a very definite title, was yet sufficient to invite a search. Accordingly I found the passage in question in the tract entitled 'De Reliquiis S. Audoeni, &c.' See the note to Art. 8, above. In the first part of this description, some slight variations occur between the MS. of Edmer in C.C.C. and those of Gervase, which I have marked below by italics. I have followed the first, and have given below that portion of the original text which belongs to the building; referring for the remainder to the Dec. Scrip. pp. 1291, 1292. It will be seen that I have taken the liberty of transposing a short sentence at the beginning of my translation, to preserve the continuity of the narrative; in other respects,

imitation of the church of the blessed Prince of the Apostles, Peter; in which his holy relics are exalted by the veneration of the whole world. The venerable Odo had translated the body of the blessed Wilfrid archbishop of York, from Ripon to Canterbury, and had worthily placed it in a more lofty receptacle, to use his own words, that is to say, in the great Altar which was constructed of rough stones and mortar, close to the wall at the eastern part of the presbytery. Afterwards another altar was placed at a convenient distance before the aforesaid altar, and dedicated in honour of our Lord Jesus Christ, at which the Divine mysteries were daily celebrated. In this altar the blessed Elphege had solemnly deposited the head of St. Swithin, which he had brought with him when he

the entire article is literally translated from the original: 'Ipsis pene diebus idem venerabilis Odo corpus beati Wilfridi pontificis Eboracensium de *rhipis* sublatum Cantuariam transtulerat, et illud in editiore entheca ut ipsemet scribit,* hoc est in majori altari quod in orientali presbiterii parte parieti contiguum de impolitis lapidibus et cemento extructum erat, digniter collocaverat. Erat enim ipsa ecclesia quod per excessum dici pacienter quæso accipiatur, sicut in historiis Beda testatur, Romanorum opere facta, et ex quadam parte ad imitationem ecclesiæ beati apostolorum principis Petri, in qua sacratissimæ reliquiæ *illius* totius orbis veneratione celebrantur decenter composita. Porro aliud altare congruo spatio antepositum prædicto altari erat dedicatum in honorem Domini nostri Jesu Christi, ubi cotidie divina mysteria *celebrabantur.* In quo altari beatus Aelfegus caput sancti Swithuni quod ipse à pontificatu Wintoniensi in archiepiscopatum Cantuariensem translatus secum tulerat, cum multis aliorum sanctorum reliquiis solenniter reposuerat. Ad hæc altaria nonnullis gradibus ascendebatur à choro cantorum *quædam cripta quam* confessionem Romani vocant. Subtus erat ad instar confessionis sancti Petri fabricata, cujus fornix eo in altum tendebatur ut superiora ejus non nisi per plures gradus possent adiri. Hæc intus ad orientem altare habebat *quod* caput beati Fursei ut antiquitas fatebatur in se habebat. Sane via una quam curvatura criptæ ipsius ad occidentem vergentem concipiebat, usque ad locum quietis beati Dunstani tendebatur, qui maceria forti ab ipsa cripta dirimebatur. Ipse namque sanctissimus pater ante ipsos gradus in magna profunditate terrræ jacebat humatus, tumba super eum in modum piramidis grandi sublimique *constructa,* habente ad caput sancti altare matutinale. Inde ad occidentem chorus psallentium in aulam ecclesiæ porrigebatur, decenti fabrica à frequentia turbæ seclusus. Dein sub medio longitudinis aulæ ipsius duæ turres erant, prominentes ultra ecclesiæ alas. Quarum una quæ in austro erat sub honore beati Gregorii papæ altare in medio sui dedicatum habebat et in latere principale ostium ecclesiæ, quod antiquitus ab Anglis et nunc usque 𝕾𝖚𝖙𝖍𝖔𝖚𝖗𝖊 dicitur, &c...'

• *Ang. Sac.,* t. ii. p. 206.

11

was translated from Winchester to Canterbury, and also many relics of other saints. To reach these altars, a certain crypt which the
Romans call a Confessionary, had to be ascended by means of several steps from the choir of the singers. This crypt was fabricated
beneath in the likeness of the confessionary of St. Peter, the vault of
whieh was raised so high, that the part above could only be reached
by many steps. Within, this crypt had at the east an altar, in which
was enclosed the head of the blessed Furseus, as of old it was asserted. Moreover, the single passage (of entrance) which ran westward
from the curved part of the crypt, reached from thence up to the
resting-place of the blessed Dunstan, which was separated from the
crypt itself by a strong wall; for that most holy father was interred
before the aforesaid steps at a great depth in the ground, and at the
head of the saint stood the matutinal altar. Thence the choir of the
singers was extended westward into the body (aula) of the church,
and shut out from the multitude by a proper enclosure.

In the next place, beyond the middle of the length of the body,
there were two towers whieh projected beyond the aisles of the
church. The south tower had an altar in the midst of it, which was
dedicated in honour of the blessed Pope Gregory. At the side was
the principal door of the church, which, as of old by the English, so
even now is called the 𝕾𝖚𝖙𝖍𝖔𝖚𝖗𝖊, and is often mentioned by this
name in the law-books of the ancient kings.[z] For all disputes from
the whole kingdom, which cannot be legally referred to the king's
court, or to the hundreds or counties, do in this place receive judgment. Opposite to this tower, and on the north, the other tower was
built in honour of the blessed Martin, and had about it cloisters
for the use of the monks. And as the first tower was devoted to legal contentions and judgments of this world, so in the, second the
younger brethren were instructed in the knowledge of the offices
of the Church, for the different seasons and hours of the day and
night.

z See a learned legal disquisition by Selden (*Dec. Script.* p. xlii).

a"The extremity of the church was adorned by the oratory of Mary, the blessed Mother of God; which was so constructed, that access could only be had to it by steps. At its eastern part, there was an altar consecrated to the worship of that Lady, which had within it the head of the blessed virgin Austroberta. When the priest performed the Divine mysteries at this altar he had his face turned to the east, towards the people who stood below. Behind him to the west, was the pontifical chair constructed with handsome workmanship, and of large stones and cement; and far removed from the Lord's table, being contiguous to the wall of the church which embraced the entire area of the building. And this was the plan of the church of Canterbury. These things we have shortly described, in order that the men of the present and future generations, when they find them mentioned in the writings of old, and perceive that the existing things do not coincide with their narratives, may know that all these old things have passed away, and that new ones have taken their place. For after the innumerable vicissitudes which this church underwent, the whole was finally consumed in our own days by fire as we have above related.

16 In the conflagration, however, by the Divine mercy and the intercession of the pious Dunstan, it happened that two houses, indispensably necessary to the existence of the brethren, remained unhurt. The refectory, namely, and the dormitory, as well as the cloisters which were attached to them.*b*

---

a 'Finis ecclesiæ ornabatur oratorio beatæ Matris Dei Mariæ. Ad quod quia structura ejus talis erat, non nisi per gradus *cuivis* patebat accessus. In cujus parte orientali erat altare in veneratione ipsius Dominæ consecratum, et in eo caput beatæ virginis Austrobertæ *honorabatur* inclusum. Ad hoc altare cum sacerdos ageret divina misteria, faciem ad populum qui deorsum stabat ad orientem versam habebat. Post se vero ad occidentem cathedram pontificalem decenti opere ex magnis lapidibus et cemento constructam, et hanc longe a Dominica mensa remotam, utpote parieti ecclesiæ qui totius templi complexio erat omnino contiguam, &c...'

b Osbern's expression is, 'so much of the cloisters as enabled them to pass from one house to the other without being wetted by rain.' 'Tantamque claustri partem sub quanta absque imbrium infusione ab una domo in aliam possent introire.' Osb. de Mirac. S. Dunst. Mabillon, t. vii. p. 695.

After this, there was ereeted over the reſting-place of the blessed man a house of small magnitude; and in this were performed daily over his holy body, masses together with the other services.[c]

17 [d]Now, after this lamentable fire, the bodies of the pontiffs (namely, Cuthbert, Bregwin, and their successors) reſted undiſturbed in their coffins for three years,[e] until that moſt energetic and honourable man, Lanfranc, abbot of Caen, was made

A.D. 1070 archbishop of Canterbury. And when he came to Canterbury, and found that the church of the Saviour, which he had undertaken to rule, was reduced to almoſt nothing by fire and ruin,

---

c 'In qua tamen conflagratione magna misericordia Dei et intercessione pii Dunſtani aċtum eſt ut due domus sine quibus fratres esse non poterant, illese ab incendio remanerent, refeċtorium videlicet ac dormitorium cum clauſtris quæ appendebant. Dehinc edificata eſt domus non adeo grandis super locum quietis beati viri et in ea circa sacrum corpus ei missæ cum reliquo servitio dei cotidie fiebant' (Ead. Mirac. S. Dunſt. MS.C.C.C. p. 160). – This book of the miracles of St. Dunſtan is the complete traċt of which Mabillon has published, from an imperfeċt copy, fragments consiſting of the beginning and the end only, without knowing the author, whom he guesses to be Osbert. In his seventh volume these fragments follow a traċt on the same subjeċt by Osbern, quoted in the laſt note.

d The proceedings of Lanfranc, which occupy this article, are related in several different works of Edmer, and others, and in each with some peculiar particulars. To avoid tautology in the text, therefore, I have amalgamated these accounts together, but have given them separately below, in their original language:

'... poſt iſtud gemendum incendium corpora pontificum supra memoratorum suis loculis immota quiescebant donec ille virorum ſtrenuissimus... Lanfrancus... Archiepiscopatu Cantuariensi funċtus eſt. Is quippe omnia quæ combuſti Monaſterii repperit vel ædificia vel ædificiorum detrita monumenta terrre coæquans et quæ sub terra erant fundamenta effodiens, cunċta nova extruxit et præfatos Antiſtites levari ac in tuto locari conſtituit; donec ea quam cœperat Ecclesia faċta esset in qua decenter poni valerent. Et ita faċtum eſt. Poſt aliquot annos in Ecclesiam jam fundatam illati sunt et in aquilonali parte super voltum singuli sub singulis locellis ligneis ubi quotidie myſterium sacrificii salutaris celebratur positi sunt.' (Edm., Vito S. Bregwini, *Ang. Sac.*, t. ii. p. 188.)

'Hic ergo Lanfrancus cum Cantuariam primò venisset et Ecclesiam Salvatoris, quam regere susceperat, incendio atq; ruinis penè nihili faċtam invenisset, mente conſternatus eſt. Sed cum magnitudo mali illum cogeret deſperare, rediit in se, animique fortitudine fretus sua commoditate poſthabita domos ad opus Monachorum necessarias, citato opere consumavit. Quibus ubi per plures annos usi sunt, adauċto eorum conventu parvæ admodum visæ sunt, Deſtruċtis itaque illis, alias decore ac magnitudine prioribus multum præſtantes rædificavit. Ædificavit et Curiam sibi, Ecclesiam præte-

he was filled with consternation. But although the magnitude of the damage had well nigh reduced him to despair, he took courage, and neglecting his own accommodation, he completed, in all haste, the houses essential to the monks. For those which had been used for many years, were found too small for the increased numbers of the convent./ He therefore pulled down to the ground all that he found of the burnt monastery, whether of buildings or the wasted remains of buildings, and, having dug out their foundations from under the earth, he constructed in their stead others, which excelled them greatly both in beauty and magnitude. He built cloisters, celerers' offices, refectories, dormitories, with all other necessary offices, and all the buildings within the enclosure of the curia, as well as the walls thereof. As for the church, which the aforesaid fire, combined with its age, had rendered completely unserviceable, he set about to destroy it utterly, and erect a more noble one. And in the space of seven years, he raised this new church from the very

rea quam spacio septem annorum a fundamentis fermè totam perfectam reddidit; in Cappis Casulis Dalmaticis Tunicis auro magnificè insignitis, palliis et aliis ornamentis multis ac præciosis nobiliter decoravit.' (Edmeri *Hist. Nov*^m. 1. i. p. 7.)

'V. Cal. Junii Obiit fœlicis memoriæ Lanfrancus Archiepiscopus,... qui istam Ecclesiam à fundamentis fundavit et consummavit... Hic etiam claustra celaria refectoria, dormitoria, cæterasque omnes officinas necessarias, et omnia ædificia infra ambitum Curiæ consistentia cum ipso ambitu mirabilater miranda ædificavit.' (Obituar. in *Ang. Sac.*, t. i. p. 55) – I omit some details concerning ornaments and books.

'Lanfrancus... Ecclesiam Salvatoris quam cum præfatum incendium tum vetustas inutilem fecerat, funditus destruere et augustiorem construere cupiens, jussit corpora sanctorum quæ in orientali parte ipsius ecclesiæ humata erant in occidentalem partem ubi memoria beatæ dei genetricis et perpetuæ virginis Marie celebris habebatur demutari. Quamobrem celebrato triduano jejunio sub innumera hominum multitudine levata sunt corpora pretiosissimorum pontificum Christi Dunstani atque Elfegi. Jam transferebantur ad destinatum locum sepulturæ et omnium ora personabant in domini laude... Itaque sacratissima corpora decentissime tumulata sunt et dies totius festivis... gaudio plenum effulsit.' (Edm., Mirac. S. Dunst., MSS. C.C.C. p. 161.) 'Testis enim est mihi ... quia cum adhuc in scholis puerulus essem &c. ...' (Edm. Epist., *Ang. Sac.*, t. ii. p. 222.)

e 'Cujus conflagrationis anno tertio... Lanfrancus... ipsam ecclesiam regendam suscepit' (Eadm. Vito S. Wilfridi, MS.C.C.C. p. 77. Mabillon, t. iii. p. 227).

f He added one hundred monks, and ordained that the total number should always be from one hundred and forty to one hundred and fifty (Gerv., Act. Pont. p. 1654).

foundations, and rendered it nearly perfect. But before the work began, he commanded that the bodies of the saints, which were buried in the eastern part of the church, should be removed to the western part, where the oratory of the blessed Virgin Mary stood. Wherefore, after a three days' fast, the bodies of those most precious priests of the Lord, Dunstan and Elphege, were raised, and in presence of an innumerable multitude, conveyed to their destined place of interment, and there decently buried. To which I, Edmer, can bear witness, for I was then a boy at the school.

18 [g]But, in process of time, as the new work of the commenced church proceeded, it became necessary to take down the remainder of the old work, where the bodies of the saints just mentioned were deposited. Having prepared, therefore, the refectory of the brethren for the celebration of Divine Service, we all proeeeded thither from the old church in festal procession, bearing with honour and reverence our glorious and sweet fathers, Dunstan and Elphege.[h]

19 [i]When the high Altar of the old church was taken down, the relics of the blessed Wilfrid were found, and placed in a coffer (scrinium); but after some years, the brethren be-

g 'Inter hæc proficiente novo opere cœptæ ecclcsiæ res exegit residuum vetusti operis, ubi memorata Sanctorum corpora erant locata subverti. Parato igitur refectorio fratrum ad divinum officium inibi celebrandum, omnes cum festiva processione illuc à veteri ecclesia perreximus præferentes cum honore et reverentia gloriosos ac dulcissimos patres nostros Dunstanum atque Elfegum.' (Edm. de Mirac. S. Dunst., MS. C.C.C. p. 163; also, Mabill., sæc. v. p.709.)

h The phrase *perreximus*, 'we proceeded,' shews that our author was present. In Mabillon's work, on account of the imperfection of the MS. which he employed, it happens that Osbern is made to relate the removal of the bodies of Dunstan and Elphege to the Lady Chapel, and Edmer (or Osbert, as he calls him), this removal to the refectory; so that the two authors seem to be relating the same event with contradictory particulars. However, in the complete MS. copy of Edmer's Miracles of St. Dunstan, these two removals are distinctly related as I have given them, and they appear to me to afford much curious information respecting the mode of conducting the operations. They give new reasons for thinking that the Saxon building was entirely eradicated; for, if it had been merely worked up into the new one, there could have been no necessity for digging the archbishops from their graves. Again, the double translation shews, that the new building occupied the same site as the old, and, also, that the work was carried on from east to west.

came of opinion that they ought to have a more permanent resting-place, and, accordingly, a sepulchre was prepared for them, on the north side of an altar, in which they were reverently inclosed, on the fourth idus of October. Moreover, when the other altars were destroyed, all the holy places, which the wisdom of the ancient fathers had constructed within them, were discovered; to the truth of which I can bear a faithful testimony, seeing that I was myself an eye-witness of all that was done.

20 *[k]*After a few years, the bodies of the pontiffs, Cuthbert, Bregwin, and their successors, were brought into the newly-founded church, and placed in the north part, upon a vault, each in a separate wooden coffin, and there, daily, the mystery of the Sacrifice of Salvation was celebrated.

21 *[l]*In our own time, it happened to one of the elder brethren of the church, Alfwin by name, who filled the office of sacrist, that he, on the night of the festival of St. Wilfrid, was

---

i '… Cum ergo prædictum altare subverteretur reliquiæ beati Wilfridi repertæ ac levatæ sunt atque in scrinio collocatæ. Verùm cùm post aliquot annos fratrum voluntas in eo consentiret, ut magis fixo loco clauderentur: sepulcrum eis in aquilonari parte altaris factum est, et in eo sunt quarto idus Octobris reverenter inclusæ' (Edm., Vito S. Wilf. MS. C.C.C. p. 77. Mabillon, t. iii. p. 227). '… Cum altaria quoo nominavimus subverterentur, sanctuaria omnia (qure in eis ut diximus antiquorum auctoritas patrum esse astruxerat) sine diminutione reperta sunt. Quæ ita se habuisse sine ulla ambiguitate fateri veraciter possum, quippe qui propriis oculis omnia cum fierent intuitus sum…' (Ead., de Reliq. MS. C.C.C. Gervase, p. 1292). The 12th of October appears in the Romish calendar as the deposition of Wilfrid. Gervase tells us below that Wilfrid was deposited behind the altar of the Trinity chapel, to the left, that is, on the north, if used with reference to a person standing in front of the altar. This deposition of Wilfrid must have taken place after the enlargement of the choir by Anselm, described below.

k 'Post aliquot annos in Ecclesiam jam fundatam illati sunt et in aquilonali parte super voltum* singuli sub singulis ligneis locellis, ubi quotidie mysterium Sacrificii salutaris celebratur positi sunt.' (Edm., Vit. Bregw., *Ang. Sac.*, t. ii. p. 188.)

l Slightly abridged from a passage in Edm., Vit. S. Wilf. MS. C.C.C. p. 86. It is contained in a sequel which has escaped Mabillon. The dream gives some useful information respecting the arrangement of the church of Lanfranc, of which more

---

* 'Lanfrancus… Sanctorum Episcoporum corpora in aquilonari parte super voltum magnum et pulcherrimum imposuit reverentur et collocavit decenter et sub singulis locellis mirifice ordinavit' (Osbern, *Ang. Sac.*, t. ii. p. 77).

resting in a certain lofty place in the church, outside the choir, and before an altar, above[m] which, at that time, the relics of the blessed Wilfrid were deposited in a shrine (feretrum). There, as he lay between sleeping and waking, he saw the church filled with light, and angelic persons performing the service, and beheld those whose duty it was to read or sing, ascend the cochlea or winding-stair, and ask a blessing before the altar and body of the blessed man, which done, they straightway descended, returned, and resumed the usual office of the church with all solemnity.

22 Archbishop Anselm, who succeeded Lanfranc, (A.D. 1093), appointed Ernulf to be prior. This Ernulf was a Frenchman,[n] and originally a monk of St. Lucian, in Beauvais. He, then, becoming dissatisfied with that monastery, joined Lanfranc, whose pupil he had been at Bec, and remained with him as a monk at Canterbury. After the death of Lanfranc, he was made prior, as above related, then (in 1107) abbot of Burgh (Peterborough), and finally (A.D. 1114), bishop of Rochester. While at Canterbury, having taken down the eastern part of the church which Lanfranc had built, he erected it so much more magnificently, that nothing like it could be seen in England, either for the brilliancy of its glass windows,

below. 'Nocte festivitatis extra chorum in quodam edito ipsius ecclesiæ loco coram altari super quod tunc temporis reliquiæ beati Wilfridi in feretro erant locatæ quiesceret, et nec plene vigilans nec plene dormiens jaceret, &c... Cumque ad lectiones et responsoria ventum esset eos qui vel legere vel cantare debebant per cocleam ascendere ac coram altari et corpore beati viri quasi pro benedictione supplicare contemplatus est. Quo facto mox redeundo descendebant et officium legendi et cantandi ubi mos est in ecclesia ipsa decentissime persolvebant.'

m 'Super,' that is, beyond or behind the altar. The eastern parts of a church were the upper (or prior) parts, and the western the lower (or posterior) parts, in the ancient nomenclature; and as the early altars were isolated, eminent saints were honoured by being deposited behind the altars, 'retro altare.'

n 'Is natione Gallus,' says Malmesbury, (de Gest. Pont. p. 224); on the contrary, according to the Annals of Rochester, he was an Englishman, 'de Anglia natus,' *Ang. Sac.*, t. i. p. 342.

o '...Cantiæ dejectam priorem partem Ecclesiæ, quam Lanfrancus ædificaverat, adeo splendide erexit, ut nihil tale possit in Anglia videri, in vitrearum fenestrarum luce, in marmorei pavimenti nitore, in diversicoloribus picturis, quæ mirantes oculos trahunt ad fastigia lacunaris' (Will. Malms., *de Gestis Pont.*, p.234). The whole article is derived from the same page.

the beauty of its marble pavement, or the many coloured pictures which led the wondering eyes to the very summit of the ceiling.[o]

23 This chancel, however, which Ernulf left unfinished, was superbly completed by his successor Conrad, who decorated it with excellent paintings, and furnished it with precious ornaments.[p] At Burgh, Ernulf pulled down the ruinous old buildings, laid new foundations, and finished them to the roof; to wit, a dormitory, chapter-house, refectory, and necessarium.[q] And at Rochester, he built a dormitory, chapter-house, and refectory.[r]

24 His works at Canterbury, however, originated with Anselm, for that prelate allowed the monks to manage their own affairs, and gave them for priors Ernulf, and then Conrad, both monks of their own monastery. And thus it happened that, in addition to the general prosperity and good order of their property, which resulted from this freedom, they were enabled to enlarge their church, by all that part which stretches from the great tower to the east; which work Anselm himself provided for. For when Duke Robert of Normandy undertook his crusade (A.D. 1096), great riches were exacted from the English by his brother King Henry to supply him with funds, and the archbishop being compelled to contribute, drew out a large sum from the treasury of the church of Canterbury. And to make amends, straightway granted to the said church the revenues of his town of Peckham, for seven years, the whole of which were expended upon the new work.[s]

p '… Cancellum quippe Ecclesiæ,… quem venerabilis Ernulphus antecessor ejus imperfectum reliquerat, ipse suà industrià magnificè consummavit, consummatumque egregia pictura decoravit, decoratum verò preciosis ornamentis locupletavit.' Obit. in *Ang. Sac.*, t. i. p. 137.

q Chron. J. Abbas, p. 61.

r Ann. Ecc. Roff., in *Angl. Sac.* t. i. p.342.

s '…Super hæc, ipsum oratorium quantum a majore turri in Orientem porrectum est ipso Patre Anselmo providente, disponente, auctum est' (Ed., *Hist. Nov.*, 1. v. p. 108). '…Et quidem eodem spatio ipsa Ecclesia eâdem villa potita est, et silva et villæ et toti redditus ejus in novo opere, quod à majori turre in orientem tenditur, quodq; ipse Pater Anselmus inchoàsse dinoscitur, consumpta sunt' (*Hist. Nov.* 1. ii. p. 35). The whole of Article 24. is derived from the *Historia Novorum*, pp. 108 and 35.

25

A.D. 1121

[t]'Not long before the death of Archbishop Radulf, a certain Teutonic monk named Lambert, who came into England under the patronage of the new queen (Adelais), visited Canterbury, and remained there for some time, residing with the brethren. He became fond of frequenting the place where the relics of the archbishops were deposited, to pray there, to celebrate masses there, and was wont to ask all manner of questions, as to who this or that one had been, and what might be the name of the one who rested in this or that coffin. At length he conceived a vehement desire to obtain the body of St. Bregwyn, and take it to his own country, intending, as he said, to construct a monastery under his patronage. He had even got the consent of the archbishop, and was making interest with the king, through the queen, for this purpose, when his own death put a stop to the matter. But the monks were set on their guard; and to make such attempts more difficult in future, they removed the relics of the above-named father, together with those of the blessed Archbishop Plegemund, to the south part of the church, and there decently entombed them behind[u] the altar

t Abridged from the narrative of Edmer (Vit. S. Bregw., *Ang. Sac.*, t. ii, p.188).

u 'Post Altare,' Edmer. ' Supra Altare,' Osbern (p. 77). See note *m*, p. 18. above.

x '...Ecclesiam Cantuariæ à Lanfranco fundatam et consummatum sed per Anselmum auctam. iiij non. Maii anno M.C. xxx. cum honore et munificentia multa dedicavit. Huic dedicationi interfuit Rex Anglorum Henricus... Rex etiam Scotiæ David interfuit præfatæ dedicationis et omnes episcopi Angliæ. Non est audita talis dedicatio in terra post dedicationem templi Salomonis.' (Gerv. Act. Pont. p. 1664.) This dedication is also mentioned by Diceto, Bromton, and Matthew Paris, but the latter historian also mentions a dedication in 1115, which, as it is not to be found in any other author, and especially not in the local historian Gervase, is probably an error. Diceto terms the church Ecc[a]. S[æ]. Trinitatis, (p. 504); and Matthew Paris (in the dedication of 1130), Ecc[a]. Christi (p. 60). It is not certain at what time the name of the Holy Trinity was bestowed on this church. Thorn employs it throughout his chronicle, even from the time of Abp. Cuthbert, probably, however, using the name by which it was known in his own time. But to the sentence of Bede (Art. 1. above), which he copies, he adds, that the church was called Christ Church from that day, and the above dedication he records by saying, 'that the church of the Holy Trinity was dedicated, which was afterwards vulgarly denominated Christ Church' (p. 1799). It is called Trinity Church in Domesday. On the other hand, Gervase always calls it Christ Church. The modern historians do not throw any light upon the matter (Vide Somner, p. 87; Battely, p.11; Dart. p. 9).

of St. Gregory. One of the monks named William, by consent of the others, undertook the management of this affair, and, by his industry and care, nearly all the funds were obtained that were required for the translation of the relics, and for the erection of the sepulchres.

26 The church of Canterbury, thus founded and finished by Lanfranc, but enlarged by Anselm, was dedicated by Arch-

A.D. 1130 bishop William, with all respect and liberality, on the 4th of May. At this dedication were present, Henry king of England, David king of Scotland, and all the bishops of England. So famous a dedication has never been heard of on the earth since the dedication of the temple of Solomon.[x]

Chapter 2

ON THE PLAN AND ARRANGEMENT OF THE SAXON CATHEDRAL

IN THE LAST CHAPTER I have endeavoured to collect in order every passage from the historians that contains the slightest allusion to the building. From these we gather that an ancient church, the work of the Romans, was by Augustine (in 602) again recovered to Christianity, that it was enlarged by Odo (about 950), and finally pulled down by Lanfranc in 1070. These facts are but scantily sufficient for a period of six centuries, and as the essential repairs of Odo are related in connexion with a monkish legend, we may fairly suspect that other facts of equal importance concerning the repairs or changes have been forgotten, because no such legend had been attached to them.

It is scarcely necessary to remark, that this building was plainly not of wood; Odo is distinctly said to have raised the walls, but whether of stone or brick does not appear. However, the expressions and details which have survived to us concerning the operations of Lanfranc, are so decided with respect to the hopeless condition and total destruction of the church when he came to the see, that I have no doubt whatever of its entire eradication at that time. Consequently it is vain to look to the present building for the slightest remains of the Saxon cathedral, and in endeavouring to form its plan, we must depend wholly upon the written description.

Fortunately, however, we owe that written description, as well as most of the allusions which are collected in the last chapter, to a writer who by his own account had seen the ruined cathedral before it was pulled down, and was himself a witness to the various operations carried on, besides being a diligent collector of traditions relating to the place.

Perhaps one of the most striking features of Edmer's description, is the statement that the church was in some sort arranged in imitation of the church of St. Peter at Rome, and as Edmer had accompanied Anselm to Rome, he was well qualified to judge of the resemblance. Accordingly the truth of this assertion appears fully borne out by comparing the two. For although the ancient Basilica of St. Peter was altogether destroyed in the sixteenth century, to make way for the existing building, yet ample particulars of it have been preserved. Plans and drawings were made before its demolition, which are still preserved in the Vatican, and which have been published by various authors, as well as minute descriptions and investigations. From these I have drawn up the short description which follows of the arrangement of St. Peter's, as far as may be necessary for the explanation of those of the Saxon church in question, referring for more ample particulars to the authorities cited below.[y]

Fig. 1. (page 25) represents a small portion of the plan of the church including the apse, part of the transept and part of the nave, and of the aisle on each side of it. But it must be added, that this church had two aisles on each side of the nave, which could not be included within the boundary of this sketch.

The pavement of the transepts was on the same level as that of the nave and its aisles. But that of the apse was raised about five feet higher,[z] forming the platform of the presbytery, which extended about nine feet into the transept.

This church, like most of the ancient churches, had its entrance at the east end, and the apse in question at the west. At the extreme west point, B, was placed the pontifical chair, upon a platform raised by several steps above the level of the presbytery. To the right

y Fontana; *Il Tempio Vaticano*, Roma, 1694. – Ciampini; *De Sacris Edificiis a Constantino Mᵒ. constructis,* Rom. 1693.—Bonanni; Templi Vatican Historia, Rom. 1700.—Costaguti e Ferrabosco; *Architettura della Basilica di S. Pietro in Vaticano,* Rom. 1684.

z These measures I have reduced to English feet; I have been obliged to trust to the scales upon the engravings, which unfortunately are often far from being precise or consistent.

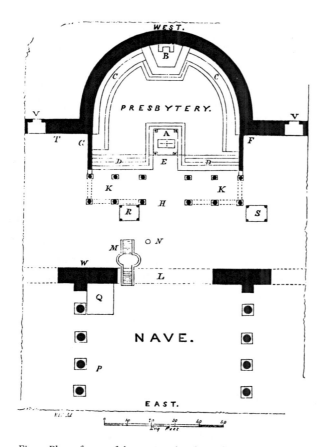

Fig. 1 Plan of part of the ancient basilica of St Peter at Rome.

and left of this chair, the walls of the apse were lined by the seats of the cardinals, at *CC*. At the edge of the platform to the east stood the high Altar *A,* under a ciborium or canopy which rested upon four pillars of porphyry, the situation of which is marked upon the plan, which also shews that this altar was raised by steps above the pavement of the presbytery. The apse itself was fifty-eight feet in diameter, and thirty-two feet in depth. On each side, a flight of five steps, *D,* led down to the transept. Beneath this platform, and close to the wall of the apse, there was a semicircular passage or vaulted crypt, which was employed as a *polyandrum,* or burial-place, and filled with the coffins of the popes. The entrances to this crypt were to the right and left of the platform of the presbytery, at *E* and *G* in the plan, for the steps, *D*, already mentioned, abutted at their extremities against a low vertical wall, in the face of which the entrances to these passages were constructed, so that persons entering at *F*, could pass completely round and come out at *G*, as Ciampini expressly states.[a]

Under the high Altar and central portion of the presbytery, was constructed the famous subterranean chapel, which was termed the confessionary (Confessio) of St. Peter.[b] The exact dimensions of this chapel have not been recorded, but some facts mentioned by ancient authors shew that it was sufficiently capacious to receive a considerable number of persons at once. There was an altar within this chapel, and in the front of the altar a small window-like opening, called the confessionary of the altar. To this opening corresponded another opening in the pavement within the altar, which looked into a small chamber or cell below it. In this cell was deposited the coffer of bronze, inclosing another of silver, which was believed to contain the remains of St. Peter. By means of these two openings the coffer could be seen, and the pallia, as also veils for the decoration of churches, golden keys, and other similar matters, could be brought into contact with it, from which ceremony they were thought to have acquired marvellous virtues, which made them acceptable gifts for archbishops and kings. This chapel had no communication with the polyandrum, and the access to it was by means of a flight of steps in front of the high Altar at *E*. These

---

a The dimensions of this passage have not been preserved, but it was evidently narrow and small. Lonigo calls it 'quel picciol luogo.' (Bonanni, p. 306.) And Ciampini terms the entrance 'angustum ostium,' p. 53.

b Confessio, the confessionary, must not be confounded with *confessionale,* the confessional, a place in which the Romish priests receive the confessions of their flock. The first is clearly defined by Du Cange as follows. '*Confessio* is a name anciently applied to the sepulchres of the Martyrs, or *Confessors,* as they were termed. Over these, altars were often placed, and hence the name was also given to the place under the high Altar, in which the relics and bodies of the Saints were enclosed.'

steps are not shewn in the plan, for it appears that at the beginning of the thirteenth century, and probably by order of Innocent III, it was thought advisable no longer to allow access to the body of St. Peter, lest some German emperor or antipope should be tempted to remove so invaluable a relic from Rome. Accordingly, the steps which led down to the chapel were removed, their place made level with the rest of the pavement, and the openings into the confessionary walled up, thus reducing the front of it to a plain vertical face. The plan therefore which, as before said, was taken in the sixteenth century, represents this new arrangement; previously to which, the front of the presbytery exhibited a descending flight of steps in the centre, with an ascending flight to right and left.[c]

In front of the steps were placed twelve columns of Parian marble, arranged in two rows. These were of a spiral form, and decorated with sculpture of vine-leaves. They were of great antiquity, and reported to have been brought from Greece, or from the temple of Solomon. Their bases were connected by lattice-work of metal, or by walls of marble, breast high, and shewn by the dotted lines, so as to enclose the space marked *K K*, which was termed the vestibule of the confessionary. The entrance to this was at *H*, between the central pillars, where the cancelli or lattices were formed into doors, which thus gave access to the presbytery, as well as to the confessionary. Above these columns were laid beams, or entablatures, upon which were placed images, candelabra, and other decorations; and, indeed, the successive popes seem to have lavished every species of decoration in gold, silver, and marblework, upon the enclosure and the crypt below. For ample details of which, I must refer to the works already quoted, as my present object is with the arrangements only. The entire height, measured to the top of the entablature, was about thirty feet. The columns, with their connecting lattices and entablature, formed, in fact, the screen of the chancel.[d]

c Similar arrangements still exist in the Roman churches of S. Prassede, and S. Lorenzo *fuori le mure,* and partly at the Lateran.

d Eight of these venerable columns were employed by Bernini in the decoration of the four upper niches of the great piers of the dome, where they may be still seen.

The nave was divided from the transept by an arch, *L*, termed the principal arch, or triumphal arch.[e] Nearly under this stood the *ambo*, or pulpit, *M*, from whence the Gospel was read to the people. The choir of the canons was a wooden structure, placed opposite one of the south pillars of the nave, at *P*. Whether this was the original position does not appear, for it is merely described as a very ancient arrangement. In the other churches of Rome it was placed in the centre of the nave, and had two *ambones*, one on the north and the other on the south, for the Epistle and Gospel respectively.[f] At *Q*, however, an oratory and altar of relics was erected by Pope Gregory III (A.D. 731–741) for the use of the canons. And it must be observed, that all the arrangements which I have described, are of great antiquity, and all existed at the time of Odo, and most of them, indeed, in the days of Augustine, and were similar to those of other churches of the same period. The confessionary and presbytery belong to the original building of Constantine and Pope Sylvester, although they were repaired by subsequent popes. Six of the columns in front were placed there by Constantine, and the other six by Gregory III. I shall merely add, that in front of the columns at *R*, Pope Paschal I (A.D. 817–824) placed an altar dedicated to Sixtus I; and that another ancient altar stood at *S*, on the spot where the bodies of St. Peter and St. Paul were originally buried. The tomb of Pope Sylvester stood at *T*, and of Pope Vigilius at *V*. The font was placed at the end of the north transept by Pope Liberius (A.D. 352–366), and was reconstructed on a larger scale by Leo III (A.D. 795–816). The end of this transept was screened off by columns and an entablature, and the font stood in the space behind them. It was circular, and surrounded by porphyry columns.

---

e Under this arch a beam was fixed, and the tympanum or space included between the soffit of the arch and the beam was occupied by a singular kind of iron lattice-work, representing a cross in the centre, and the keys on each side. The antiquity of this arrangement is not recorded, but it corresponds to the rood-beam.

f For example: the Lateran, S. Maria Maggiore, S. Lorenzo *fuori le mure*, S. Clemente, S. Maria in Cosmedin, &c.

The description of the Saxon church of Canterbury (in Art. 15) will be found to coincide with the above of St. Peter at Rome, in several particulars: 1. The crypt evidently extends only under the presbytery or altar end of the church, and not under the choir of the singers; 2. This crypt has an altar within, and a single entrance in the middle of its western face. That the floor of this Saxon crypt was not on the same level with that of the choir, is shewn by the wall which is said to have separated it from the grave of Dunstan: for Dunstan was buried before the steps, and in a grave six feet beneath the pavement. Now, if the floor of the crypt was four or five feet below that of this pavement, its western wall behind and under the steps, may naturally be said to have separated the crypt from his grave; but this phrase would hardly have been either necessary or applicable, if the pavements within and without the crypt had been at the same elevation. Moreover, Edmer tells us that the altar-platform was ascended by a *few* steps from the pavement. But if the crypt had been entirely above the level of the pavement, *many* steps would have been required, for the crypt must, at least, have been high enough for a man to stand upright in; 3. The matutinal altar, which seems to have been employed by the monks in their daily service, was placed below the platform of the presbytery, and in front of the steps, a position analagous to the altars shewn in the plan of St. Peter's, due allowance being made for the enormous magnitude of the latter. No mention is made of any outer crypt behind the principal one, and similar to the polyandrum of St. Peter's. But such a circumscribing crypt has been discovered in the ancient Saxon church of Brixworth, running, however, outside the apse; 4. The choir of the singers is extended in our Saxon church into the nave; an arrangement perfectly analogous to those of the Roman basilicas, and like them it was probably enclosed by a breast-high wall, which was intended to keep off the laity, without preventing their view of the ceremonies.

Fig. 2. will serve to make my explanation of the plan of the Saxon cathedral more intelligible.

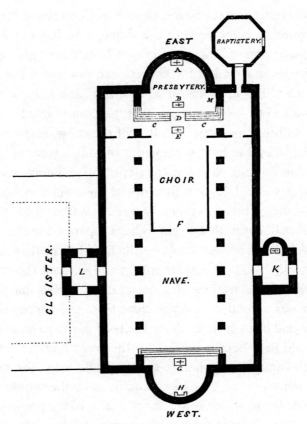

Fig. 2 Plan of the Saxon cathedral of Canterbury.

Edmer's description plainly mentions the body or *aula* of the church and its aisles, but is silent with regard to a transept. That it had a circular termination or apse, may be gathered from the use of the word *curvatura,* in the crypt, and from analogy with its model, St. Peter's at Rome, as well as other churches of the period. Now, although the large Basilicas of Rome have transepts, yet in the lesser ones the building is a plain parallelogram, of which the aisles extend from end to end, and the divisions of the church are made out upon its floor by steps and partitions, but do not shew themselves in the external form. Thus in the oft-quoted example of St. Clemente, the transept is traced within by a low transverse partition, which runs immediately in front and below the steps of the presbytery, cutting off a strip at the altar end, which rises in the aisles a step or two above the general level; and the choir, in like manner, is formed by breast-high partitions, which enclose a parallelogram, less in breadth than the central alley of the *aula*, or body, into which this enclosed space extends, and occupies about half its length.

The phrase employed by Edmer in describing this *chorus* or choir of the singers, which he says extended into the body of the church, has induced me to follow the model of St. Clement in the plan, (fig. 2), which must of course be looked upon as a mere diagram.

The platform of the presbytery (or upper floor of the crypt, to use the phraseology of Edmer's description), may be supposed to extend, in imitation of that of St. Peter, in front of the apse. The front boundary will be formed by two lateral ascending flights of steps, C C, having between them in the centre the descending flight into the crypt, at D; and the position of the tomb of Dunstan is distinctly defined to be at the western end of this passage, and therefore in the central line of the plan, and of course sufficiently in advance of the steps to allow access to them, while the matutinal altar being at the head of the saint, is therefore at the west end of his tomb at E.

On the platform of the presbytery at the extreme east point, A, was the high Altar enclosing the body of St. Wilfrid, and at B, in front of it, the Altar of Christ, where mass was daily celebrated. Edmer tells us, in his Life of Wilfrid (Art. 7), that Archbishop Odo deposited his relics in the great Altar which was consecrated to Christ; but in his description of the Saxon church (Art. 13), this author relates that the relics were deposited in the great Altar which was close to the eastern wall of the presbytery, and which was built of rough stones and cement, and that afterwards another altar was set before this, and dedicated to Christ for the daily mass. The rude construction especially mentioned, indicates the venerable antiquity of the first altar, and the subsequent addition of another altar for daily use, seems to shew that the first was now considered too sacred for the ordinary priests, and that like the high Altar of St. Peter and some others at Rome, at which the pope only officiates on great festivals, this was reserved in a similar way. The second altar, *B*, was perhaps erected by Archbishop Elphege, the fourth after Dunstan, as he is said to have enclosed in it so many relics. The position of the high Altar is different from the usual disposition of the period, which places it on the spot occupied by the second altar, *B*, namely, in front of the presbytery.

The tomb of Odo was on the south side of the Altar of the Saviour (about *M*); *E, F,* is the probable extent of the choir of the singers. About or beyond the middle of the body of the church were two towers, *K, L; K* had an altar, and also seemed to have served as a porch to the church. The altar therefore was probably in an apse. The tower, *L,* on the north side may have formed a part of the cloister, as I have shewn it, or it may have stood in one angle of the cloister; the use to which it was put, namely, to teach the younger brethren, was common to all the cloisters. As for the Lady-chapel, so minutely and curiously described by our author, we are told that it was raised above the level by steps, that the altar was at the east end, and therefore in front of the steps, *G,* and that the officiating priest turned his face to the people below, while standing at this altar. The altar must therefore have been between him and the people; and the people must also have been without the boundary of the chapel and in the body of the church. Hence I conclude this chapel to have been a mere apse as I have drawn it, and as the episcopal throne was at its western extremity, *H,* it becomes very probable that this was in fact the original altar end of the church, and that like most of the ancient churches, including St. Peter's, it was at first built with its altar at the west end.[g]

g Churches that have been thus turned from west to east, are to be found on the continent exhibiting ancient apses at the west end, and more recent ones at the east. The cathedral of Nevers and the church of St. Benoit at Paris (now used as the theatre of the Pantheon), are French examples; Germany will furnish several others, and at Rome we may cite the Basilica of S. Lorenzo.

Of the Baptistery, or church of St. John, erected by Archbishop Cuthbert, no particulars have been preserved except the meagre notice that it stood at the east of the great church, and nearly touched it. It was not, therefore, a chapel branching from it. I have sketched an octagon in the plan from analogy merely with other examples.[h]

As to the history of these arrangements of the church, we can offer little beyond conjecture; Edmer describes it as he knew it, and had seen it during its demolition; and we know that Odo raised the walls when he made a new roof, and that this operation took up three years, a period which seems to imply a considerable work, if indeed the time has not been exaggerated to give importance to the miracle. However, the church of Brixworth has plainly had its walls raised, and a clerestory with windows added, even in the Saxon period; assuming that midwall balustre-shafts are to be received as characteristic of this period; for a triple window with such shafts was inserted in the western wall when the walls were so raised. By analogy then, we may guess that Odo gave to his church a clerestory which it had not before. But whether the said church was the ancient Roman Christian building, or whether Augustine or one of his successors might not have rebuilt it, who can tell. The communication with Rome was always maintained in these early centuries, and the imitation of St. Peter's was as likely to have been an object with Odo or with Augustine, as to have resulted from the original plan and derivation of the building and its site from the primitive Christianity of the island. That the Saxons did imitate Roman models is shewn by the very mid wall shafts of the Saxon windows which are directly copied from those of the Roman Campanili.

It was a part of the policy of Augustine, acting under the advice of Pope Gregory, not to destroy the heathen temples, but only the idols therein; and to consecrate their buildings to Christianity,

---

h The Baptistery of Constantine stands in a somewhat similar relative position to the church of the Lateran, but at a greater distance. The Baptistery of St. Peter's was at the end of the north transept, as already mentioned.

that the people might the more readily be induced to worship according to the new doctrines, because the buildings were familiar to them as houses of prayer; similar motives would operate much more strongly in favour of preserving the old Christian church; and I do not, therefore, think it probable that it was rebuilt by Augustine, whatever his successors might have done during the three centuries that separated him from Odo. But as all this is but vain conjecture, I shall conclude this chapter, reserving the discussion of Lanfranc's building and its subsequent enlargement, to follow the tract of Gervase, to which I must now introduce my readers.

Chapter 3

HERE BEGINNETH GERVASE HIS HISTORY OF THE BURNING
AND REPAIR OF THE CHURCH OF CANTERBURY

This Chapter is literally translated from the tract of Gervase, and
contains the whole of it, with the omission only of a long digression upon the merits of Thomas à Becket, and of a quotation from
the Opuscula of Edmer, which I have already given in its proper
place in the first chapter. I have broken the original into sections,
for the convenience of reference, and have also added, within parentheses, letters referring to my plans and sections.

1. The Conflagration

IN THE YEAR OF GRACE[i] one thousand one hundred and seventy-
four, by the just but occult judgment of God, the church of Christ
at Canterbury was consumed by fire, in the forty-fourth year from
its dedication,[k] that glorious choir, to wit, which had been so magnificently completed by the care and industry of Prior Conrad.

Now the manner of the burning and repair was as follows. In
A.D. 1174, the aforesaid year, on the nones of September, at about the
Sep. 5
between ninth hour, and during an extraordinarily violent south
3 and 4
P.M. wind, a fire broke out before the gate of the church, and outside the walls of the monastery, by which three cottages were half
destroyed. From thence, while the citizens were assembling and
subduing the fire, cinders and sparks carried aloft by the high wind,
were deposited upon the church, and being driven by the fury of
the wind between the joints of the lead, remained there amongst

i This chronological term, 'the year of grace,' was invented by Gervase himself. The
years so termed correspond to our years of our Lord, with the difference only that
they begin from Christmas Day (vide Chron. Gervasii, p. 1337, also see *l'Art de Verifier
les Dates*).

k For it was dedicated in 1130 (Art. 26. chap. i).

the half rotten planks, and shortly glowing with increasing heat, set fire to the rotten rafters; from these the fire was communicated to the larger beams and their braces, no one yet perceiving or helping. For the well-painted ceiling below, and the sheet-lead covering above, concealed between them the fire that had arisen within.

Meantime the three cottages, whence the mischief had arisen, being destroyed, and the popular excitement having subsided, everybody went home again, while the neglected church was consuming with internal fire unknown to all. But beams and braces burning, the flames rose to the slopes of the roof; and the sheets of lead yielded to the increasing heat and began to melt. Thus the raging wind, finding a freer entrance, increased the fury of the fire; and the flames beginning to shew themselves, a cry arose in the church-yard: 'See! see! the church is on fire.'

Then the people and the monks assemble in haste, they draw water, they brandish their hatchets, they run up the stairs, full of eagerness to save the church, already, alas! beyond their help. But when they reach the roof and perceive' the black smoke and scorching flames that pervade it throughout, they abandon the attempt in despair, and thinking only of their own safety, make all haste to descend.

And now that the fire had loosened the beams from the pegs that bound them together, the half-burnt timbers fell into the choir below upon the seats of the monks; the seats, consisting of a great mass of wood-work, caught fire, and thus the mischief grew worse and worse. And it was marvellous, though sad, to behold how that glorious choir itself fed and assisted the fire that was destroying it. For the flames multiplied by this mass of timber, and extending upwards full fifteen cubits,' scorched and burnt the walls, and more especially injured the columns of the church.

And now the people ran to the ornaments of the church, and began to tear down the pallia and curtains, some that they might save,

c About 25 feet.

but some to steal them. The reliquary chests were thrown down from the high beam and thus broken, and their contents scattered; but the monks collected them and carefully preserved them from the fire. Some there were, who, inflamed with a wicked and diabolical cupidity, feared not to appropriate to themselves the things of the church, which they had saved from the fire.

In this manner the house of God, hitherto delightful as a paradise of pleasures, was now made a despicable heap of ashes, reduced to a dreary wilderness, and laid open to all the injuries of the weather.

The people were astonished that the Almighty should suffer such things, and maddened with excess of grief and perplexity, they tore their hair and beat the walls and pavement of the church with their heads and hands, blaspheming the Lord and His saints, the patrons of the church; and many, both of laity and monks, would rather have laid down their lives than that the church should have so miserably perished.

For not only was the choir consumed in the fire, but also the infirmary, with the chapel of St. Mary, and several other offices in the court; moreover many ornaments and goods of the church were reduced to ashes.

2. The Operations of the First Year.

Bethink thee now what mighty grief oppressed the hearts of the sons of the Church under this great tribulation; I verily believe the afflictions of Canterbury were no less than those of Jerusalem of old, and their wailings were as the lamentations of Jeremiah; neither can mind conceive, or words express, or writing teach, their grief and anguish. Truly that they might alleviate their miseries with a little consolation, they put together as well as they could, an altar and station in the nave of the church, where they might wail and howl, rather than sing, the diurnal and nocturnal services. Meanwhile the patron saints of the church, St. Dunstan and St. Elfege, had their resting-place in that wilderness. Lest, therefore, they should suffer even the slightest injury from the rains and storms, the monks, weeping and lamenting with incredible grief and anguish, opened the tombs of the saints and extricated them in their coffins from the choir, but with the greatest difficulty and labour, as if the saints themselves resisted the change.

They disposed them as decently as they could at the altar of the Holy Cross in the nave. Thus, like as the children of Israel were ejected from the land of promise, yea, even from a paradise of delight, that it might be like people, like priest, and that the stones of the sanctuary might be poured out at the corners of the streets;[d] so the brethren remained in grief and sorrow for five years in the nave of the church, separated from the people only by a low wall.

Meantime the brotherhood sought counsel as to how and in what manner the burnt church might be repaired, but without success; for the columns of the church, commonly termed the pillars, were exceedingly weakened by the heat of the fire, and were scaling in pieces and hardly able to stand, so that they frightened even the wisest out of their wits.

French and English artificers were therefore summoned, but even these differed in opinion. On the one hand, some undertook to repair the aforesaid columns without mischief to the walls above. On the other hand, there were some who asserted that the whole church must be pulled down if the monks wished to exist in safety. This opinion, true as it was, excruciated the monks with grief, and no wonder, for how could they hope that so great a work should be completed in their days by any human ingenuity.

However, amongst the other workmen there had come a certain William of Sens,[e] a man active and ready, and as a workman most

d Hos. iv. 9; Lam. iv. 1.

e Sens is a considerable town of France, 84 miles S.E. of Paris, in the ancient province of Champagne. The nave of its cathedral, which was completed about 1168, has several peculiarities in common with the work of Canterbury, of which more below.

skilful both in wood and stone. Him, therefore, they retained, on account of his lively genius and good reputation, and dismissed the others. And to him, and to the providence of God was the execution of the work committed.

And he, residing many days with the monks and carefully surveying the burnt walls in their upper and lower parts, within and without, did yet for some time conceal what he found necessary to be done, lest the truth should kill them in their present state of pusillanimity.

But he went on preparing all things that were needful for the work, either of himself or by the agency of others. And when he found that the monks began to be somewhat comforted, he ventured to confess that the pillars rent with the fire and all that they supported must be destroyed if the monks wished to have a safe and excellent building. At length they agreed, being convinced by reason and wishing to have the work as good as he promised, and above all things to live in security; thus they consented patiently, if not willingly, to the destruction of the choir.

And now he addressed himself to the procuring of stone from beyond sea. He constructed ingenious machines for loading and unloading ships, and for drawing cement and stones. He delivered molds for shaping the stones to the sculptors who were assembled, and diligently prepared other things of the same kind. The choir thus condemned to destruction was pulled down, and nothing else was done in this year.

As the new work is of a different fashion from the old, it may be well to describe the old work first and then the new. Edmer, the venerable singer, in his Opuscula, describes the ancient church built in the Roman manner, which Archbishop Lanfranc, when he came to the see, utterly destroyed, finding it in ashes. For Christ Church is recorded to have suffered thrice from fire; first, when the blessed martyr Elfege was captured by the Danes and recived the crown of martyrdom; secondly, when Lanfranc, abbot of Caen, took the rule of the church of Canterbury; thirdly, in the days of Archbishop Richard and Prior Odo. Of this last conflagration, unhappily, we have not read, but have seen it with our own eyes.[f]

3. Of the Church of Lanfranc

I will first describe the work of Lanfranc; beginning from the great tower, not because the whole of this church has been destroyed, but because part of it has been altered. The tower, raised upon great pillars (*AAAA*, fig. 3, next page), is placed in the midst of the church, like the centre in the middle of a circle. It had on its apex (*pinna*) a gilt cherub.[g] On the west of the tower is the nave or *aula* of the church, supported on either side upon eight pillars.[h] Two lofty towers (*B C*) with gilded pinnacles terminate this nave or aula. A gilded *corona*[i] hangs in the midst of the church. A screen with a loft (*pulpitum*) (*DD*), separated in a manner the aforesaid tower from the nave, and had in the middle, and on the side towards the nave, the altar of the holy cross (*E*). Above the *pulpitum,* and placed across the church, was the beam, which sustained a great cross, two cherubim, and the images of St. Mary, and St. John the Apostle. In the north aisle (*ala*) was the oratory and altar of St. Mary (*F*).[j] In this nave, as

f Here Gervase inserts Edmer's description of the old church, which I have already given in its proper place, and need not therefore repeat (See Art. 15, chap. 1 above). The two previous conflagrations have been abundantly described in our first chapter (Articles 12 and 14), but this distinct enumeration of them from the pen of a local historian is valuable because it shews that there were three and no more.

g This central tower retained the name of Angel steeple to the last.

h I have numbered the pillars in the plan. Our author's description is so precise, and so consistent, that the mere addition of a plan, and of the letters of reference in parentheses, is sufficient to make it intelligible.

i Probably a 'corona lucis,' or chandelier, as in the choir.

j The position of this Lady chapel is determined by a fact mentioned by Somner. He says, 'Archbishop Richard, Becket's immediate successor, was buried there. I have it from the church records, verified by the leaden inscription and pontifical relicks, to wit, his cope,crosier, and chalice, lately found in digging Dr. Anian's grave by Sir John Boys his monument on the north side of the body toward the upper end.' (p. 92.) By the church records he probably means Gervase his Acts of the Archbishops, where we find (p. 1675) that Archbishop Richard was buried 'in ecclesia Christi in oratorio

Fig. 4 Plan of the crypt of Trinity chapel.

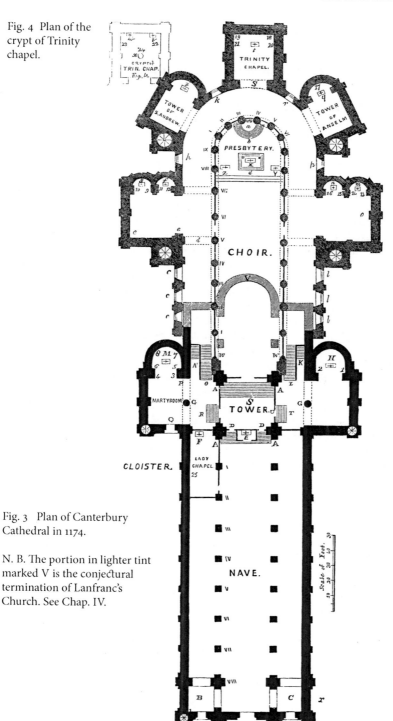

Fig. 3 Plan of Canterbury Cathedral in 1174.

N. B. The portion in lighter tint marked V is the conjectural termination of Lanfranc's Church. See Chap. IV.

above related, we for five years endured banishment. The aforesaid great tower had a cross[k] from each side, to wit, a south cross and a north cross, each of which had in the midſt a ſtrong pillar; this

beatæ Mariæ.' Archbishop Theodbald was translated thither when the Trinity chapel was taken down (Gervase, below). Sir John Boys was buried in the laſt severey but one, at 25 in the plan.

k Transept.

l In Norman cathedrals this pillar in the transept suſtaining a kind of gallery is not unusual. It occurs in St. Stephen's at Caen, the abbey at Cerisy, the abbey at Fécamp, the cathedral at Seez, and S. George de Boscherville. At Fécamp and Seez the arches are pointed. Cotman has a good view of the example at S. George de Bocherville, in his *Normandy*, which muſt have been very similar to the arrangement described in the text. In our own country good ſpecimens remain in the transepts of Wincheſter, and in those of Ely. The latter is erecſted upon more pillars and set closer to the wall than usual (Vide Cotman's *Normandy*, p. 5; Britton and Winkles' *Wincheſter*, &c...). The place of these columns is marked *G* in the plan.

The position I have given them correſponds to that of the similar columns in St. Stephen's at Caen; a church which, as I shall presently shew, is the same as the present in its plan and dimensions.

m The Latin word which I have conſtantly rendered *apse* is *porticus*. This word has various meanings, and has thus given rise to much confusion in the translation of architecſtural descriptions. In its classical sense it is a covered walk with an open colonnade at the side, whence it passed to the aisles of a church, and to the porch of entrance. In the present description, wherever Gervase inserts a *porticus* I find an *apse* in the building, and as the latter was one of the senses in which the word in question was employed, I have uniformly so translated it. In the glossary of Elfric (p. 78) we find ABSIDA, ſinepealt cleoſa vel poſtic, that is, *a round chapel or porticus*. And Somner renders the Saxon word poſtice by 'porticus, absis, a porch, the circling or embowing of an arch or vault.'

LIST OF THE ALTARS IN FIG. 3.

NAVE AND TRANSEPTS CRYPT	EAST OF THE GREAT TOWER (cont.)
E Holy Cross.	**f** S. Stephen.................S. Nicholas.
F S. Mary the Virgin.	**g** S. Martin ....S. Mary Magdalen.
H S. Michael, *below.*	**i** S. Andrew ....Innocents.
All Saints, *above.*	**m** S. Gregory.................S. Audoen.
M S. Blaise, *above*	**n** S. John Evangeliſt....S. Paulinus.
S. Benedicſt, *below.*	**o** S. Katherine.
	q SS. Peter and Paul ...(S. Gabriel.)
EAST OF THE GREAT TOWER	**t** Holy Trinity.
X High Altar.................The Virgin Mary.	**v** S. Auguſtine (Archbp.)
Y S. Dunſtan.	**w** S. John Baptiſt.
Z S. Elfege.	

(pillar) sustained a vault which proceeded from the walls on three of its sides;[l] the plan of the one cross is exactly the same as that of the other. The south cross was employed to carry the organ upon the vault. Above and beneath the vault was an apse(*H*),[m] extended towards the east. In the lower part was the altar of St. Michael, in the upper part the altar of All Saints. Before the altar of St. Michael to the south was buried Archbishop Feologild (1).[n] On the north the holy virgin Siburgis (2), who for her sanctity was buried in the church by St. Dunstan.

Between this apse and the choir the space is divided into two, that is, for the few steps (*K*) by which the crypt is gained, and for the many steps (*L*) by which the upper parts of the church are reached. The north cross similarly had two apses (*M*). In the upper one is the altar of St. Blasius, in the lower that of St. Benedict. In this lower one, to the right of the entrance, was buried Archbishop William (3), who

S. Gabriel's altar is not mentioned by Gervase, but is known by the ancient painting and inscription which still remains.

n The monuments are numbered with Arabic numerals, as in the following list.

Burial places of Archbishops of Canterbury in Plan, fig. 3, in the order of their succession to the see.

11	Cuthbert	12		26	Siric	crypt
12	Bregwin	13		27	Elfric	16
14	Athelard	11		28	Elfege	Z
15	Vulfred	9		29	Living	10
16	Feologild	1		30	Egelnoth	5
17	Chelnoth	8		31	Eadsin	23
18	Athelred	22		34	Lanfranc	20
19	Plegemund	14		35	Anselm	17
20	Adhelm	7		36	Radulph	4
21	Vulfelm	6		37	William Corboil	3
22	Odo	18		38	Theobald	21
24	Dunstan	Y		39	Thomas à Becket	24
25	Ethelgar	15		40	Richard	25

This list shews that Gervase has accounted for the places of all those archbishops which were buried in Christ Church, for the only missing numbers in the order of succession are (13) Jambert, who was buried at St. Augustine's, (23) Elsin, who died abroad, and (32, 33) Robert and Stigand, who were both ejected from their offices. The following numbers refer to the burial places of other persons. Siburgis, at 2; S. Wilfrid of York, at 19; and Queen Ediva, at or near *o*, in the south transept.

with great glory dedicated the church of Christ which I am describing. He also founded the church of St. Martin for monks of Dover. To the left lies the predecessor of William, Archbishop Radulf (4), who, although discreet in wisdom and of renowned eloquence, yet did Pope Calixtus prefer before him Thurstan, archbishop of York, and Hugo, abbot of St. Augustine. In the same apse, before the altar on the right, lies Archbishop Egelnoth (5), and to the left Vulfelm (6). Behind the altar to the right Adhelm (7), to the left Chelnoth (8). And thus is the aforesaid apse graced. Between this apse and the choir the space is divided into two, that is, for the steps (N) which descend to the crypt, and for the steps (O) which serve those who ascend to the eastern parts of the church.

Between this space and the aforesaid apse is a solid wall (P), before which that glorious companion of martyrs, and guest of the Apostles, the holy Thomas, fell in the body by the swords of raging men, but transmitted his unconquered soul to heaven to be straightway crowned with the glory and honour of the eternal kingdom.[o] This place of martyrdom is opposite to the door of the cloister (Q)

[o] This account of the locality of Becket's fall agrees perfectly with the particulars furnished by other authorities. Thus Gervase in his Chronicle relates that the monks were at vespers, and that the archbishop entered the church (of course through his cloister door Q), for the purpose of attending the service; that he had ascended a few steps (probably those at O) when his four assailants entered from the cloister and enquired for him. He coming down the steps which he had ascended, confronted his enemies, and after exchanging words of defiance with them, most minutely recorded by the historian, was struck and fell, exclaiming, 'To God and S. Mary, to S. Denys and the patron saints of the church, I commend myself and the cause of the church.'[*] Diceto adds that his body lay on the pavement to the right of the altar of St. Benedict (M), which is also quite consistent with the statement in our text, that he fell in front of the wall (P). Matthew Paris, and others, in more general terms relate that he was slain before the altar of St. Benedict. Our text goes on to mention an altar raised on the 'locus martyrii,' that is, against the wall P, and the demolition of the pillar G, and the vault above it. And the flat wall is to this day preserved, for the masonry of the fifteenth century, which clothes every other part of the transept, does not intrude itself here, but is cut off many feet above. Erasmus was shewn in this transept, 'an altar of wood, consecrated to the Virgin, small and only worth seeing as a monument of antiquity, reproving by its simplicity the luxury of his time. There the pious man was said to have bad farewell to the Virgin when at the point of death, and there they kept

[*] Gerv. Chon. p. 1146. Diceto, p. 556.

by which those four notaries of the devil entered that they might stamp the seal of the genuine prerogative of the martyr between the anvil and hammer, that is, that they might adorn the head of St. Thomas, prostrate between the pavement and their swords, with the stamp of the Most High, the chaplet of martyrdom.*p*

The pillar (G) which stood in the midst of this cross, as well as the vault which rested on it, were taken down in process of time out of respect for the martyr, that the altar, elevated on the place of the martyrdom, might be seen from a greater distance. Around and at the height of the aforesaid vault a passage was constructed from which pallia and curtains might be suspended.*q* From the cross to the tower, and from the tower to the choir many steps (R S) ascended. There was a descent (T) from the tower into the south cross by a new entrance (U). Also a descent from the tower to the nave through two doors (DD). Thus much for the church of Lanfranc. Now let us describe the choir, lest the memory thereof be utterly lost.

4. Of the Choir of Conrad

I have described, as shortly as I might, the church constructed by Archbishop Lanfranc; that is, the nave, crosses, towers, and their appurtenances. Still the actual sight of them will explain them as much more rapidly as it will effectually.

You must know however, good reader, that I never saw the choir of Lanfranc, neither have I been able to meet with any description of it.*r* Edmer, indeed, describes the old church, which before the time

---

as a relic the point of the sword with which he was struck.' Gervase says it broke upon the pavement. This therefore was the altar at P.

p I have translated this characteristic rhapsody as closely as I was able.

q When this vault was destroyed the chapel of St. Blaise must have lost 'its convenient access. Accordingly the body of the Saint was removed, for in a list of relics in Prior Henry de Estrias's register (MSS. Cott. Galba E. iv. f. 122) we find, 'Corpus S. Blasii in feretro retro magnum altare.' See chap. 6. below.

r Gervase was at Canterbury in 1170, the year of Becket's murder, and the choir of Lanfranc was pulled down about seventy years before. In this time it seems that all tradition of its arrangement had vanished.

of Lanfranc was constructed after the Roman manner. Also he mentions, but does not describe, the work of Lanfranc which succeeded this old church, and the choir of Conrad constructed in the time of St. Anselm. Now, therefore, that this choir of Conrad, so gloriously completed, has been in our own days miserably consumed by fire; my poor and simple pen shall attempt its description, lest the memory of so great a man and so noble a work be utterly lost. And although my purpose is not to describe the mere arrangement of stones, yet it is impossible clearly to shew the places of the Saints and of their repose, which are in various parts of the church, without first describing the building itself in which they were arranged, under the inspection and with the assistance of their historian Edmer. Let us begin therefore with the aforesaid great tower, which, as already explained, is placed in the midst of the whole church, and proceed eastward. The eastern pillars of the tower projected as a solid wall, and were formed each into a round semi-pillar (*W*). Hence in line and order were nine pillars[s] on each side of the choir, nearly equidistant from each other; after these six[t] in a circuit were arranged circularly, that is, from the ninth on the south side to the ninth on the north, of which the two extreme ones were united by the same one arch. Upon these pillars, as well those in the straight line as those in the circuit, arches were turned from pillar to pillar; above these the solid wall was set with small blank windows. This wall (on either side), bounding the choir, met the corresponding one at the head of the church in that circuit of pillars.[u] Above the wall was the passage which is called *triforium*,[v] and the upper windows. This was the termination upwards of the

s Numbered in the plan in order, with Roman numerals.

t Also numbered in the plan. The architectural arrangements of the arches, galleries, and windows, will be fully discussed in the next chapter.

u The end of the church where the high Altar stood, was commonly termed the *Caput Ecclesiæ,* or *Capitium,* and sometimes the *Capitulum,* although the latter word was more commonly appropriated to the Chapter House. (Vide Du Cange, under the above words.)

v Our author is the only ancient authority for the use of the word 'triforium'; and it is clear that he employs it in a different sense from that which is now given to it, and which has been derived from the hasty interpretation of Gervase by some modern

interior wall. Upon it rested the roof and a ceiling decorated with excellent painting. At the bases of the pillars there was a wall built of marble slabs, which, surrounding the choir and presbytery, divided the body of the church from its sides, which are called aisles (*alœ*).

This wall inclosed the choir of the monks, the presbytery, the great Altar (*X*) dedicated in the name of Jesus Christ, the altar of St. Dunstan (*Y*), and the altar of St. Elfege (*Z*), with their holy bodies.

Above the wall,[x] in the circuit behind and opposite to the altar, was the patriarchal seat (*a*) formed out of a single stone, in which, according to the custom of the Church on high festivals, the archbishops were wont to sit during the solemnities of the mass, until the consecration of the Sacrament; they then descended to the Altar of Christ by eight steps (*a b*).

From the choir to the presbytery there were three steps (*Z Y*) ; from the pavement of the presbytery to the altar three steps (*d*); but to the patriarchal seat eight steps (*b a*). At the eastern horns of the altar were two wooden columns, gracefully ornamented with gold and silver, and sustaining a great beam, the extremities of which rested upon the capitals of two of the pillars (ix, ix).[y] This beam,

writers. The universal sense in which the triforium is now taken, is for the compartment that in many churches exists between the pier-arches and the clerestory windows, whether that compartment have a passage or no. But it will appear from our author's use of the word, that it has no especial reference to this compartment, but is employed solely in the sense of an upper passage or thoroughfare, perhaps confined to a covered passage, in opposition to *alura*, which meant any kind of passage; but it was certainly not confined to passages in the thickness of the wall, because the lower triforium of Canterbury passes over the side-aisle vaults; while the upper one, which would now be called the clerestory gallery, is formed in the thickness of the wall, as will be shewn in the next chapter. Somner imagines the word to be a corruption or Latinization of 'thoroughfare,' which doubtless exactly expresses its meaning. But the modern sense has now received the sanction of such excellent writers, and is in itself so useful and expressive, that I have no wish to disturb it, and when I use it myself, in the following pages, shall follow their example, although in translating I must use it as my author does.

x The wall was evidently low, from its construction of marble slabs, and the chair, elevated upon eight steps, would rise above it.

y In the plan the altar is inadvertently set a little too far westward. The pillars ix, ix, and the columns behind the altar should be in one straight line.

carried across the church above the altar, and decorated with gold, sustained the representation of the Lord (*majestatem Domini*), the images of St. Dunstan and of St. Elfege, together with seven chests (*scrinia*), covered with gold and silver, and filled with the relics of divers saints. Between the columns there stood a gilded cross, of which the cross itself was surrounded by a row of sixty transparent crystals. In the crypt, under this altar of Christ, stood the altar of the holy Virgin Mary, to whose honor the entire crypt was dedicated. Which crypt occupied precisely the same space and compass in length and breadth as did the choir above it. In the midst of the choir hung a gilded corona carrying four and twenty wax lights. This was the fashion of the choir and presbytery. But the exterior wall of the aisles was as follows. Beginning from the martyrium of St. Thomas, that is to say from the cross of Lanfranc, and proceeding towards the east as far as the upper cross, the wall contained three windows (*c c c*), and no more. Opposite to the fifth pillar of the choir, the wall received an arch (*d*) from it, and turning towards the north (*e e*) it formed the north cross. The breadth of this cross extended from the fifth to the seventh pillar. For the wall proceeding northwards from the seventh pillar as from the fifth, and making two apses (*f g*), completed the cross of the eastern part. In its southern apse (*f*) was the altar of St. Stephen, under which, in the crypt, was the altar of St. Nicholas. In the northern apse (*g*) was the altar of St. Martin; and under it, in the crypt, the altar of St. Mary Magdalene. At the altar of St. Martin two archbishops were laid, to the right Vulfred (9), to the left Living (10); and similarly at the altar of St. Stephen, to the left Athelard (11), and to the right the venerable Cuthbert (12).

[2]He it was who, being endowed with great wisdom, procured for Christ Church the right of free sepulture. For the bodies not only of the archbishops, but of all who died in the city, were wont, from the time of St. Augustine, to be carried to the church of the Apostles Peter and Paul, without the city, and there buried. For in those days it was said that the city was for the living and not for the dead. But

the blessed Cuthbert was grieved to think that after death he must be separated from his church and his children, that in life were the delights of his affection. Wherefore he sought and obtained from Rome the right of free burial for Christ Church. He was the first who, by the will of God, the authority of the high pontiff, and the permission of the king of England, was buried in Christ Church, and so also were all his successors, save one alone named Jambert.

From this apse of St. Stephen, the aforesaid wall proceeding eastward had a window (*h*) opposite to the side of the great Altar (*X*). Next after came a lofty tower, placed as it were outside the said wall, which was called the tower of St. Andrew because of the altar of St. Andrew (*i*) which was therein, below which, in the crypt, was the altar of the Innocents. From this tower the wall proceeding, slightly curved and opening into a window (*k*) reached a chapel, which was extended towards the east at the front*a* of the church, and opposite to the high seat of the archbishop. But as there are many things to be said of the interior of this chapel, it will be better to pause before its entrance until the south wall with its appurtenances has been traced up to the same point. This south wall, beginning from the apse of St. Michael (*H*) in the cross of Lanfranc, reaches the upper cross after three windows (*l l l*). This cross at its eastern side, like the other, had two apses. In the southern apse (*m*) was the altar of St. Gregory, where two holy archbishops were deposited; to the

---

z See Chap. 1. Art. 3, where a similar passage is translated from this author's Acts of the Archbishops.

a We have seen above that *Caput*, the 'head' of the church, was exclusively applied to the altar end thereof. *Frons*, the 'front,' however, can be shewn by many examples to have been employed for *either end* of the building. In the present case the east end is clearly meant, and in the Registrum Roffense there occurs a gift of four windows 'in fronte versus majus altare' (p. 124), and other examples might be quoted. Mr. Dennewas, I believe, the first to point out this application of the word, (Thorpe's *Custumale*, p. 171.) On the other hand, the following examples selected out of many will shew that it was also employed for other extremitios of the building' 'edificavit navem ecclesiæ… a turre chori usque ad frontem,' (Swapham 99). 'Opus frontale nostræ ecclesiæ,' namely (from the context), the west end of the nave of St. Alban's. (Matt. Par. 1054.)

south St. Bregwin (13), to the north St. Plegemund (14), underneath in the crypt was the altar of St. Audoen, archbishop of Rouen. In the other apse (*n*) was the altar of St. John the Evangelist, where two archbishops reposed; to the right Ethelgar (15); to the left Elfric (16); underneath in the crypt was the altar of St. Paulinus, where Archbishop Siric was buried. Before the altar of St. Audoen and nearly in the middle of the floor was the altar of St. Katherine (*o*). The wall proceeding from the above cross had a window (*p*) opposite to the great Altar, and next a lofty tower, in which was the altar of the Apostles Peter and Paul (*q*).

But St. Anselm (17) having been translated there and placed behind the altar gave his name to the altar and to the tower. From this tower the wall proceeding for a short space and opening into a window (*r*) in its curve, arrived at the aforesaid chapel of the Holy Trinity, which was placed at the front of the church. An arch (*s*) springing from each wall, that is, from the south and from the north, completed the circuit.

The chapel[b] placed outside the wall but joined to it and extended towards the east, had the altar of the Holy Trinity (*t*), where the blessed martyr Thomas celebrated his first mass on the day of his consecration. In this chapel, before and after his exile, he was wont to celebrate mass, to hear service, and frequently to pray. Behind the altar there lay two archbishops, to the right St. Odo (18), to the left St. Wilfrid (19), archbishop of York; to the south, close to the wall, the venerable Archbishop Lanfranc (20), and to the north Theodbald (21). In the crypt (see fig. 4) beneath, there were two altars, on the south (*v*) that of St. Augustine, the apostle of the English, and on the north (*w*) that of St. John Baptist. Close to the south wall Archbishop Ethelred (22) was deposited, and Eadsin (23) against the north wall.

In the middle of this chapel there stood a column (*x*) which sustained arches and a vault, that came from all sides. At the base of this

b In the ancient drawing of the monastery of Christ Church by Edwyn the Scribe, this chapel is shewn and without an apse. As the apses are carefully put in in many other parts of this drawing, I have followed this authority, and laid down the chapel square in fig. 3.

column, on the eastern side,... was the place (24) where the blessed martyr Thomas was buried, on the day after his martyrdom...[c]

And now the description, as concise as I could make it, of the church which we are going to pull down, has brought us to the tomb of the martyr, which was at the end of the church; let therefore the church and the description come to an end together; for although this description has already extended itself to a greater length than was proposed, yet many things have been carefully omitted for the sake of brevity. Who could write all the turnings, and windings, and appendages of such and so great a church as this was? Leaving out, therefore, all that is not absolutely necessary, let us boldly prepare for the destruction of this old work and the marvellous building of the new, and let us see what our master William has been doing in the meanwhile.

5. Operations of the First Five Years

[d]The Master began, as I stated long ago, to prepare all things necessary for ther new work, and to destroy the old. In this way the

Sep. 6, 1174, to   first year was taken up. In the following year, that is, after
Sep. 5, 1175   the feast of St. Bertin (Sep. 5, 1175), before the winter, he

c Here our author indulges in a long digression concerning the merits and miracles of Thomas à Becket, which contains no information, direct or indirect, about the building, and I therefore pass it over. To make amends for this omission we may take the following particulars of his costume from our circumstantial author's Acts of the Archbishops. The blessed martyr suffered in the ninth year of his patriarchate, on the 4th kalend of January 3rd feria (Tuesday Dec. 29.) while the monks were singing vespers, and in the year of our Lord, 1170. His body was placed in a feretrum, and laid before the Altar of Christ. On the morrow the brethren carried him into the crypt, and placed him in a marble sarcophagus; and that I may truly relate what I saw with my eyes and handled with my hands, he wore next to his skin a hair shirt (*cilicium*), then a linen one (*staminiam*), over these the black cowl (*cucullam nigram*), then the alb in which he was consecrated; the tunic also and dalmatic, the chasuble, pall, and mitre. Below he had hair drawers (*femoralia cilicina*) with linen ones over, woollen hose and sandals.' Gerv. Act. Pont. Cant., p. 1673.

d This account of the progress of the works will be rendered more intelligible by a reference to the plan, fig. 5, and the section fig. 6, assisted by the following summary. (p. 54, footnote).

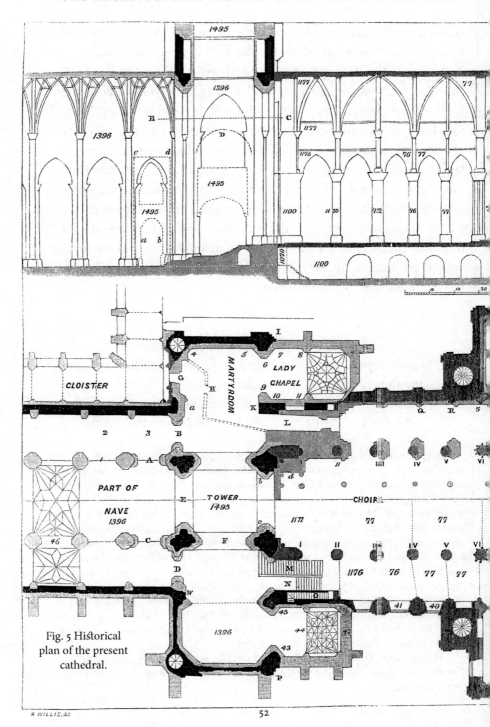

Fig. 5 Historical plan of the present cathedral.

R WILLIS. del

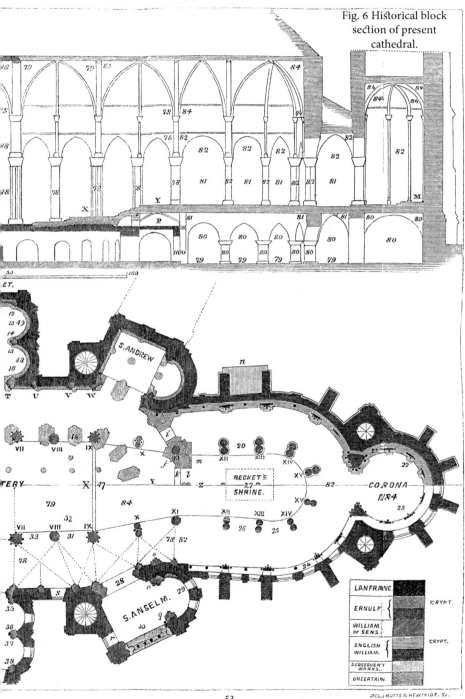

Fig. 6 Historical block section of present cathedral.

erected four pillars, that is, two on each side, and after the winter two more were placed, so that on each side were three in order, upon which and upon the exterior wall of the aisles he framed seemly arches and a vault, that is, three *claves*[e] on each side. I put *clavis* for the whole *ciborium* because the *clavis* placed in the middle locks up and binds together the parts which converge to it from every side. With these works the second year was occupied.

In the third year he placed two pillars on each side, the two extreme

A.D. 1176

SUMMARY OF THE WORKS IN EACH YEAR							
Archi- tects	Years	CHOIR AND TRINITY CHAPEL				Crypt of Trinity Chapel	Corona	Other works
		Pillars	Side vaults	Triforia and clerestories	Upper vaults			
William of Sens	1175	I . III						
	1176	IV	I....IV					
	1177	V VI	IV...VI	I....VI	I....VI			
	1178	VII..XI	VII..XI	VII..XI	VI. VII and tran- septs			
English William	1179				VII..IX	outer wall to window sills		transept finished
	1180					outer wall to vault spring pillars XII ...XV	crypt and its vault	choir fitted up old Trinity chapel demol- ished
	1181					crypt finished		outer walls of Trinity chapel to the capitals
	1182	XII..XV	XI....XV				to base of clerestory	outer win- dows of Trinity chapel finished
	1184			XI .. XV	IX..XV		cler. win- dows and vault	All roofed in

The Roman numerals refer to the pillars in plan, fig. 5. When employed for the vaults they will be readily understood to mean those vaults which extend from pillar to pillar. The longitudinal section (fig. 6.) which accompanies this plan is drawn in block only, that is, omitting all small details, and even the arches of the triforium and clerestory. The numbers upon this section are either dates at length, or the two last figures of the date, thus 75 for 1175, and so on. Also the pillars and side walls are dated separately, and for the side vaults, triforia and clerestories, and upper vaults, the date figure is placed at each end of the work of each year.

ones of which he decorated with marble columns placed around
_{A.D. 117⁶⁄₇} them, and because at that place the choir and crosses were to
meet, he conſtituted these principal pillars. To which, having
added the key-ſtones and vault, he intermingled the lower triforium from the great tower to the aforesaid pillars, that is, as far as the
cross, with many marble columns. Over which he adjuſted another
triforiumᶠ of other materials, and also the upper windows. And in
the next place, three *claves* of the great vault, from the tower, namely, as far as the crosses. All which things appeared to us and to all
who saw them, incomparable and moſt worthy of praise. And at so
glorious a beginning we rejoiced and conceived good hopes of the
end, and provided for the acceleration of the work with diligence
and ſpirit. Thus was the third year occupied and the beginning of
the fourth.ᵍ

e Each compartment of a vault was frequently termed, in later times, a 'severy.' As
for example, in the contraċts for King's College chapel, and in William of Worceſter
(p. 244), and sometimes ſpelt 'civery,' (Will. of Worc., p. 302.) But Gervase, in the
above passage uses' ciborium' in this sense. Now the *ciborium* is properly the canopy
of the high Altar, which is supported upon four pillars, and which is usually vaulted
in one compartment. Thus each compartment of a vault resembles a *ciborium,* and
a vaulted aisle may be compared to a series of ciboria. Du Cange informs us that in
Auvergne, *cibory* is used for a vaulted tomb. Apparently, therefore, severey is a corruption of ciborium, and is not derived from the verb 'to sever,' as might at firſt sight
be supposed.

Clavis and *Key* are, in medieval architeċture, the bosses of a ribbed vault; (vide
Architeċtural Nomenclature of the Middle Ages, p. 43.)

f In modern language 'the clereſtory gallery.' See note at pp. 46–7 above.

g In the annals of these operations, it is clear that the years of which Gervase ſpeaks
are made to begin on the 6th of September, namely, the morrow of St. Bertin, for
the fire happened on St. Bertin's day, the 5th of September, 1174. At the end of the
firſt year's operations he goes on to say as above. 'In the following year, that is, *after
the feaſt of St. Bertin,* such and such works were done before the winter, and such
and such works after the winter.' But in winding up his enumeration of the works of
the *third* year, he employs the phrase, 'In iſtis igitur annus tercius completus eſt, et
quartus sumpsit initium.' 'The third year was thus filled up and the fourth had also begun;' by which he means to include the small remaining time between Sep. 5, (1177)
of the third year of operation, and the period when the winter of 1177 put a ſtop to
the works. This appears from the absence of any mention of works before the winter,
and from his beginning his account of the fourth year's operations with the summer.
It is necessary clearly to underſtand this in order to make the time of the maſter's

In the summer of which, commencing from the cross, he erected ten pillars, that is, on each side five. Of which the two first

were ornamented with marble columns to correspond with the other two principal ones. Upon these ten he placed the arches and vaults. And having, in the next place, completed on both sides the triforia and upper windows, he was, at the beginning of the fifth year, in the act of preparing with machines for the turning of the great vault, when suddenly the beams broke under his feet, and he fell to the ground, stones and timbers accompanying his fall, from the height of the capitals of the upper vault, that is to say, of fifty feet. Thus sorely bruised by the blows from the beams and stones, he was rendered helpless alike to himself and for the work, but no other person than himself was in the least injured. Against the master only was this vengeance of God or spite of the devil directed.

The master, thus hurt, remained in his bed for some time under medical care in expectation of recovering, but was deceived

accident and the remaining works intelligible, for the same phrase is used in winding up the fourth year's accounts, and for all the subsequent ones, so that, in truth, after the three first years the works are really enumerated from their beginning in each summer to the time when the following winter suspends them, and I have therefore inserted in the margin the date of one year only to each after the third. The master's fall must have happened shortly after the 13th of September, 1178, to have allowed time for the works that were done between his fall and the winter. The eclipse is described in his peculiar manner by Gervase in his Chronicle: I subjoin the passage. He seems to insinuate above that the eclipse was the forerunner of the mischief, but is ashamed to confess that he thought so. 'In the month of September, on the Vigil of the

A.D. 1178,
Sept. 13,
between
12 and 2
o'clock

Holy Cross, on the fourth day of the week, and on the 27th day of the moon, at about the sixth hour, there was an eclipse of the sun in Kent, not total, but partial. For the body of the sun appeared horned, with the horns turned westward, like the moon when she is twenty days old. The remainder of the sun's circumference was not to be seen. For a certain black sphere covered the splendour of the sun, and gradually descending, caused the horned brightness to revolve around its upper part, until its points hung down and looked towards the earth. But as that black thing slowly pursued its course, these horns, which were first turned to the west, now pointed to the east, as in the new moon. And then the black sphere passed away, and the sun resumed his brightness. The sky being for a little while covered with mist assisted the sight in observing these things. Meanwhile the air was in many places tinted with various hues, of red, yellow, green, and paleness. All which was seen by me, and by most of the dwellers in Kent.' (Chron. Gerv. p. 1445.)

in this hope, for his health amended not. Nevertheless, as the winter approached, and it was necessary to finish the upper vault, he gave charge of the work to a certain ingenious and industrious monk, who was the overseer of the masons; an appointment whence much envy and malice arose, because it made this young man appear more skilful than richer and more powerful ones. But the master reclining in bed commanded all things that should be done in order. And thus was completed the ciborium between the four principal pillars. In the key-stone of this ciborium the choir and crosses seem as it were to meet. Two ciboria on each side[h] were formed before the winter; when heavy rains beginning stopped the work. In these operations the fourth year was occupied and the beginning of the fifth. But on the eighth day from the said fourth year, on the idus of September, there happened an eclipse of the sun at about the sixth hour, and before the master's accident.[i]

And the master, perceiving that he derived no benefit from the physicians, gave up the work, and crossing the sea, returned to his home in France. And another succeeded him in the charge of the works; William by name, English by nation, small in body, but in workmanship of many kinds acute and honest. He in the summer
A.D. 1179. of the fifth year finished the cross on each side, that is, the south and the north, and turned the ciborium which is above the great Altar, which the rains of the previous year had hindered, although all was prepared. Moreover, he laid the foundation for the enlargement of the church at the eastern part, because a chapel of St. Thomas was to be built there.

For this was the place assigned to him; namely, the chapel of the Holy Trinity, where he celebrated his first mass, where he was wont to prostrate himself with tears and prayers, under whose crypt for so many years he was buried, where God for his merits

[h] Namely, the vaults of the eastern transepts.
[i] The text here appears to be corrupted; but the true sense of the passage must be as I have given it.

had performed so many miracles, where poor and rich, kings and princes, had worshipped him, and whence the sound of his praises had gone forth into all lands.

The master William began, on account of these foundations, to dig in the cemetery of the monks, from whence he was compelled to disturb the bones of many holy monks. These were carefully collected and deposited in a large trench, in that corner which is between the chapel and the south side of the infirmary house. Having, therefore, formed a most substantial foundation for the exterior wall with stone and cement, he erected the wall of the crypt as high as the bases of the windows.

Thus was the fifth year employed and the beginning of the sixth.

6. The Entry into the New Choir

A.D. 1180   In the beginning of the sixth year from the fire, and at the time when the works were resumed, the monks were seized with a violent longing to prepare the choir, so that they might enter it at the coming Easter. And the master, perceiving their desires, set himself manfully to work, to satisfy the wishes of the convent. He constructed, with all diligence, the wall which encloses the choir and presbytery. He erected the three altars of the presbytery. He carefully prepared a resting-place for St. Dunstan and St. Elfege. A wooden wall to keep out the weather was set up transversely between the penultimate pillars^j at the eastern part, and had three glass windows in it.

The choir, thus hardly completed even with the greatest labour and diligence, the monks were resolved to enter on Easter Eve with

---

j Between the pillars IX. These are the last but two. But the penultimate vault over IX...XI. was not yet erected; and this position of the wooden wall left room to erect the steps and vault (P), which are in connection with the vault of the Trinity chapel, and probably were not built until that was finished.

the new fire.[k] As all that was required could not be fully performed on the Saturday because of the solemnities of that sacred day, it became necessary that our holy fathers and patrons, St. Dunstan and St. Elfege, the co-exiles of the monks, should be transferred to the new choir beforehand. Prior Alan, therefore, taking with him nine of the brethren of the church in whom he could trust, went by night to the tombs of the saints, that he might not be incommoded by a crowd, and having locked the doors of the church, he commanded the stone-work that enclosed them to be taken down.

The monks and servants of the church therefore, in obedience to the Prior's commands, took the structure to pieces, opened the stone coffins of the saints, and bore their relics to the *vestiarium*. Then, having removed the cloths in which they had been wrapped, and which were half consumed from age and rottenness, they covered them with other and more handsome palls, and bound them with linen bands. They bore the saints, thus prepared, to their altars, and deposited them in wooden chests, covered within and without with lead; which chests, thus lead-covered, and strongly bound with iron, were enclosed in stone-work that was consolidated with melted lead.[l] Queen Ediva also, who had been placed under the altar of the

k Cum novo igne, that is, with the lighting of the pascal candle, which was solemnly lighted on Easter Eve, and allowed to burn till Ascension Day. See the note in the next page.

l We owe many curious particulars respecting this shrine of St. Dunstan, to a correspondence printed in the *Anglia Sacra.* The monks of Glastonbury had long asserted that the body of Dunstan, after the sack of Canterbury by the Danes, was taken up and carried to Glastonbury, where accordingly they always exhibited a coffin which they asserted to contain his relics. But at the beginning of the fourteenth century they constructed a new and magnificent shrine in their church, and solemnly translated the said relics thither, to the great wrath of the monks of Canterbury. The archbishop and prior, W. Warham and Th. Goldston, immediately caused their own shrine of Dunstan to be opened, in which they found the remains of a human body, in the costume of an archbishop, with a plate of lead on his breast, inscribed with the name of Sanctus Dunstanus; and a most characteristic correspondence ensued, in which the abbot of Glaston endeavours to explain, that perhaps part only of the relics of the saint were conveyed thither; and that at all events the people had believed in the genuineness of their saint so long that he is afraid to tell them the truth. However, these documents supply many curious particulars of the arrangement of the shrine at Canterbury, from which I select the following (*Ang. Sac.,* t. ii. p. 227).

holy cross after the fire, was similarly conveyed to the vestiarium. These things were done on the night preceding the fifth feria before

_{Wednesday} the holy Easter; that is, on the sixteenth calend of May. On _{night, Ap. 16.} the morrow, however, when this translation of the saints became known to the whole convent, they were exceedingly astonished and indignant that it should have been done without their consent, for they had intended that the translation of the fathers should have been performed with great and devout solemnity.

They cited the prior and those who were with him, before the venerable Archbishop Richard, to answer for the slight thus presumptuously cast upon themselves and the holy patrons of the church, and endeavoured to compel the prior and his assistants to renounce their offices. But by the intervention of the archbishop and other men of authority, and after due apology and repentance, the convent was appeased ; and harmony being thus restored, the service of Holy Saturday was performed in the chapter-house, because the station of the monks and the altar which had been in the nave of the church, were removed to prepare for the solemnities of the following Easter Sunday. About the sixth hour the archbishop in cope and mitre, and the convent in albs, according to the custom of the church, went in procession to the new fire, and having consecrated it, proceeded towards the new choir with the appointed hymn.^m At the door of the church (Q, fig. 3) which opens to the

---

_{Ap. 20,} The shrine (feretrum) was on the 20 south of the high Altar, and erected ₁₅₀₈ in the fashion of a tomb. When it was opened, they found a chest (arca) of wood covered and lined with lead throughout, and nailed with the nails so close together, that there was not a handbreadth between them. And the length of the chest was as the length of the stone-work in which it was deposited and immersed, namely, seven feet; and it was about a foot and a half in breadth, and bound round with iron bands in every part. Within this chest was a second one (cista) of lead, not plain, but of beautiful plaited work ('Quæ quidem cista facta est non ex plano plumbo sed arte quadam pulcherrimè est plicata'). This contained a third leaden chest somewhat decayed, and in which the body was enclosed.

m These ceremonies for Easter Eve are detailed at length in the statutes of Lanfranc. The fire from whence the pascal candle in the choir was to be lighted, was made in the cloister, and the monks went in procession from the choir thither, and having consecrated the fire, they lighted a taper from it, which was ready prepared at the end

martyrium of St. Thomas, the archbishop reverently received from a monk the pix, with the Eucharist, which was usually suspended over the great Altar. This he carried to the great Altar of the new choir. Thus our Lord went before us into Galilee, that is, in our transmigration to the new church. The remainder of the offices that appertain to the day were devoutly celebrated. And then the pontiff, standing at the Altar and vested with the infula, began the Te Deum laudamus; and the bells ringing, the convent took up the song with great joy, and shedding sweet tears, they praised God with voice and heart for all His benefits.[n]

The convent was ejected by the fire from the choir, even as Adam from paradise, in the year of the Lord 1174, in the month of September, on the fifth day of the month, and about the ninth hour. They remained in the nave of the church five years, seven months, and thirteen days. And returned into the new choir in the year of grace 1180, in the month of April, on the nineteenth day of the month, at about the ninth hour of Easter Eve.

7. Remaining operations of the sixth year

Our craftsman had erected outside the choir four altars, where the bodies of the holy archbishops were deposited, as they were of old,

A.D. 1180 and as we have above described.[o] At the altar of St. Martin; Living, and Wilfrid. At the altar of St. Stephen; Athelard,

---

of a long stick (*hasta*), and carried this back to the choir with psalms and hymns and incense to light the pascal candle. (Vide Statuta Lanfranci, § 4. They are printed in Reyner's *Apostolatus Benedictinorum in Anglia*, p. 223, and in Wilkins' *Concilia*. The *Inventor rutili* of the Latin text of Gervase is the beginning of the appointed hymn.) 'Cereus Paschalis continere debet ccc. libras. ceræ.' Claud. c. 6. Battely, App. 45.

n In this year, on the 22nd of May, the church was again in peril of fire: Gervase gives this account; 'On the eleventh kalend of June the city of Canterbury was wasted by fire, many houses were already consumed, and the peril was menacing the church of the Holy Trinity, but the monks bore the shrine (feretrum) of St. Audoen to oppose the fire, when suddenly the roaring flames fled backwards from the Divine virtue as from before a wind, and presumed not to advance further.' Chron. Gervasii, p. 1457.

o Page 48 above.

and Cuthbert. In the south cross at the altar of St. John; Elfric, and Ethelgar. At the altar of St. Gregory; Bregwin, and Plegemund. But Queen Ediva, who before the fire reposed under a gilded *feretrum* in nearly the middle of the south cross, was now deposited at the altar of St. Martin, under the *feretrum* of Living.

Moreover, in the same summer, that is of the sixth year, the outer wall round the chapel of St. Thomas, begun before the winter, was elevated as far as the turning of the vault. But the master had begun a tower at the eastern part outside the circuit of the wall as it were, the lower vault of which was completed before the winter.

The chapel of the Holy Trinity above mentioned was then levelled to the ground; this had hitherto remained untouched out of reverence to St. Thomas, who was buried in the crypt. But the saints who reposed in the upper part of the chapel were translated elsewhere, and lest the memory of what was then done should be lost, I will record somewhat thereof. On the eighth idus of July the altar of the Holy Trinity was broken up, and from its materials the altar of St. John the Apostle was made; I mention this lest the history of the holy stone should be lost upon which St. Thomas celebrated his first mass, and many times after performed the divine offices. The stone structure which was behind this altar was taken to pieces. Here, as before said, St. Odo and St. Wilfrid reposed for a long period.[p] These saints were raised in their leaden coffins (*capsis plumbeis*) and carried into the choir. St. Odo, in his coffin, was placed under the feretrum of St. Dunstan, and St. Wilfrid under the feretrum of St. Elphege.[q]

[p] See p. 16 above.

[q] As a temporary resting-place only, for in the list of relics (Cott. MSS. Galba E. IV. fol. 122) we find 'Corpus S. adonis in feretro, ael coronam versus austrum. Corpus S. Wilfridi in feretro *ad coronam* versus aquilionem.' The tower mentioned above, which terminates the eastern part, was termed 'Corona S. Thomæ,' and here these two ancient relics were finally deposited. The name appears in Hollar's plan, and the tower is still called ' Becket's Crown.' In Ducange we find, 'CORONA ECCLESIÆ. Pars Templi choro postica, quod ea pars fere desinat in circulum. Charta anni 1170 in Tabulario B. Mariæ de Charitate: *Duo altaria in Corona Ecclesiæ.*' Ducange (or rather his Editor)

Fig. 7 Triforium of the choir from within.

Archbishop Lanfranc was found enclosed in a very heavy sheet of lead, in which, from the day of his first burial up to that day, he had rested untouched, in mitre and pall, for sixty-nine years and some months. He was carried to the vestiarium in his leaden covering, and there deposited until the community should decide what should be done with so great a Father. When they opened the tomb of Archbishop Theodbald, which was built of marble slabs, and came to his sarcophagus, the monks who were present expecting to find his body reduced to dust, brought wine and water to wash his bones. But when the lid of the sarcophagus was raised, he was found

thus takes the word to mean the principal apse of a church. At all events it was a general term, and not peculiar to Christ Church, Canterbury. The notion that this round chapel was called Becket's Crown, because part of his skull was preserved here as a relic (Somner, 94; Gostling, 124; Dart, 19), appears wholly untenable.

entire and rigid, and still subsisting in bones and nerves, skin and flesh, but somewhat attenuated. The bystanders marvelled at this sight, and placing him upon a bier (*tabulam gestatoriam*), they carried him as they had done Lanfranc, to the vestiarium, to await the decision of the convent. But the rumour began to spread among the people, and already, for this unwonted incorruption, many called him St. Theodbald. He was exhibited to some who desired to see him, and they helped to spread the tale among the rest.

He was thus raised from his sepulchre in the nineteenth year from his death, his body being incorrupted, and his silk vestments entire. And by the decision of the convent was buried in a leaden coffin (*in arca plumbea*) before the altar of St. Mary, in the nave of the church, which place he had wished for while living. The marble tomb was put together over him, as it was before. But Lanfranc having remained, as before said, untouched for sixty-nine years, his very bones were consumed with rottenness, and nearly all reduced to powder. The length of time, the damp vestments, the natural frigidity of the lead, and above all, the frailty of the human structure, had conspired to produce this corruption. But the larger bones, with the remaining dust, were collected in a leaden coffer (*in capsa plumbea*), and deposited at the altar of St. Martin. The two archbishops who lay to the right and left of St. Thomas in the crypt were taken up, and placed for the time in their leaden coffins (*capsis*) under the altar of St. Mary, in the crypt.

The translation of these Fathers having been thus effected, the chapel, together with its crypt, was destroyed to the very ground: only that the translation of St. Thomas was reserved until the completion of his chapel. For it was fitting and manifest that such a translation should be most solemn and public. In the mean time, therefore, a wooden chapel, sufficiently for the place and occasion, was prepared around and above his tomb. Outside of this a foundation was laid of stones and cement, upon which eight pillars of the new crypt, with their capitals, were completed. The master also carefully opened an entrance from the old to the new crypt.

Fig. 8 Arches in south aisle.

And thus the sixth year was employed, and part of the seventh. But before I follow the works of this seventh year, it may not be amiss to recapitulate some of the previous ones which have either been omitted from negligence or purposely for the sake of brevity.

8. Explanations[r]

It has been above stated, that after the fire nearly all the old portions of the choir were destroyed and changed into somewhat new and of a more noble fashion. The differences between the two works may now be enumerated. The pillars of the old and new work are alike in form and thickness but different in length. For the new pillars were elongated by almost twelve feet. In the old capitals the work was plain, in the new ones exquisite in sculpture. There the circuit of the choir had twenty-two pillars,[s] here are twenty-eight. There the arches and every thing else was plain, or sculptured with an axe and not with a chisel.[t] But here

r This section will be fully discussed in the next chapter.
r This section will be fully discussed in the next chapter.
s This number of twenty-two pillars appears to he in direct contradiction to the plan and to his own previous enumeration of nine on each side in a straight line, and six in a circuit (p. 42), which amount to twenty-four. In this passage, however, he hlts evidently omitted the two intermediate pillars (marked VI. fig. 3.), which were removed in the reconstruction of the church.
t The arches represented in figure 8 (above) occur in the south aisle, and furnish an excellent commentary to the above passage. The left hand one is similar to all the remaining arches of Ernulf's work, and its ornament has manifestly been wrought with an *axe*. The right hand arch, which resembles those of the eastern transept, the work of William of Sens, has deep moldings and the Early English dog-tooth, which could

Fig. 9 Capital of choir, south side.

Fig. 10 Capital of choir, north side.

almost throughout is appropriate sculpture. No marble columns were there, but here are innumerable ones. There, in the circuit around the choir, the vaults were plain, but here they are arch-ribbed and have keystones. There a wall set upon pillars divided the crosses from the choir, but here the crosses are separated from the choir by no such partition, and converge together in one keystone, which is placed in

Fig. 11 Capital of semi-pillar
(*W* fig. 3).

the middle of the great vault which rests on the four principal pillars. There, there was a ceiling of wood decorated with excellent painting, but here is a vault beautifully constructed of stone and light tufa. There, was a single triforium, but here are two in the choir and a third in the aisle of the church. All which will be better understood from inspection than by any description.

This must be made known, however, that the new work is higher than the old by so much as the upper windows of the body of the choir, as well as of its aisles, are raised above the marble tabling.

And as in future ages it may be doubtful why the breadth which was given to the choir next the tower should be so much contracted at the head of the church, it may not be useless to explain the causes thereof. "One reason is, that the two towers of St. Anselm and of St. Andrew, placed in the circuit on each side of the old church, would not allow the breadth of the choir to proceed in the direct line. Another reason is, that it was agreed upon and necessary that the chapel of St. Thomas should be erected at the head of the church, where the chapel of the Holy Trinity stood, and this was much narrower than the choir.

The master, therefore, not choosing to pull down the said towers, and being unable to move them entire, set out the breadth of the choir in a straight line, as far as the beginning of the towers (I...IX). Then, receding slightly on either side from the towers, and preserving as much as he could the breadth of the passage outside the choir on account of the processions which were there frequently passing, he gradually and obliquely drew in his work, so that from opposite the altar (IX), it might begin to contract, and from thence, at the third pillar (XI), might be so narrowed as to coincide with the breadth of the chapel, which was named of the Holy Trinity. Beyond these, four pillars (XII, XIII) were set on the sides at the same distance as the last, but of a different form; and beyond these other four (XIV, XV) were arranged in a circle, and upon these the superposed work (of each side) was brought together and terminated. This is the arrangement of the pillars.

The outer wall, which extends from the aforesaid towers, first proceeds in a straight line, is then bent into a curve, and thus in

---

u The plan fig. 5 will make this explanation clear, for which purpose I have inserted the Roman numerals into the text which refer to the pillars in this plan. As the upper half of this plan contains, in a lighter tint, the plan of the crypt also, which is the same as that of the old choir of Conrad, the differences will be more easily understood between the old and new choirs. The walls of St. Thomas's chapel are not parallel, but diverge slightly, as shewn by the dotted line which exactly represents the plan of the upper wall. This is parallel to the corresponding one from XI to XII, divergent from XII to XIII, and then passes round rather more than a semicircle.

the round tower the wall on each side comes together in one, and is there ended. All which may be more clearly and pleasantly seen by the eyes than taught in writing. But this much was said that the differences between the old and new work might be made manifest.

9. Operations of the Seventh, Eighth, and Tenth Years

Now let us carefully examine what were the works of our mason in

A.D. 1181 this seventh year from the fire, which, in short, included the completion of the new and handsome crypt,[x] and above the crypt the exterior walls of the aisles up to their marble capitals. The windows, however, the master was neither willing nor able to turn, on account of the approaching rains. Neither did he erect the interior pillars. Thus was the seventh year finished, and the eighth begun.

In this eighth year the master erected eight interior pillars, (XII...XV), and turned the arches and the vault with the windows

A.D. 1182 in the circuit. He also raised the tower up to the bases of

A.D. 1183 the highest windows under the vault. In the ninth year no

A.D. 1184 work was done for want of funds. In the tenth year the upper windows of the tower, together with the vault, were finished. Upon the pillars was placed a lower and an upper triforium, with windows and the great vault. Also was made the upper roof where the cross stands aloft, and the roof of the aisles as far as the laying of the lead. The tower was covered in, and many other things done this year. In which year Baldwin bishop of Worcester was elected to the rule of the church of Canterbury on the eighteenth kalend of January, and was enthroned there on the feast of St. Dunstan next after...

HERE ENDETH GERVASE HIS HISTORY OF THE BURNING AND REPAIR

OF THE CHURCH OF CANTERBURY.

x Namely, the crypt of St. Thomas's chapel, now called by its old name of Trinity chapel.

Gervase concludes his narrative of the rebuilding somewhat abruptly; and to complete this period of the history a few remarks may be necessary. The expenses of this magnificent work seem to have been partly supplied from the oblations at the tomb of St. Thomas. Battely states that three bulls still remain in the archives, concerning the oblations made at the great Altar, at the altar of St. Thomas, and the other altars, by which the convent had leave to expend all the oblations in lights and vestments for the service of the church, and in the repair of the fabric, &c; and all historians record the visits of royal and noble personages io this saint, and their liberal offerings. The translation of the body of St. Thomas from the tomb beneath to the shrine in the chapel took place on the 7th of July, A.D. 1220, with the greatest solemnity and rejoicing, the king himself being present. No dedication of the new choir is recorded. Battely seems to imagine that it was dedicated at the time of the translation to St. Thomas the Martyr, but with no sufficient authority. Dart, indeed, contradicting Battely, says that there was merely an altar dedicated to St. Thomas in the chapel of the Holy Trinity, but that the church, in all the donatives afterwards, even to the time of Henry IV, is called by the name of Christ Church, and no other. (See Battely, p. 18; and Dart, p. 12; and note x, p. 20 above.) There is some ground for supposing that the chapel, which, as we have seen was erected on the site of that of the Holy Trinity, was dedicated to St. Thomas, for it is always called the Chapel of St. Thomas. Gervase so designates it, and it is even so described in Hollar's plan. Now, however, it has resumed its ancient title of the Trinity Chapel, under which I shall generally mention it.

Chapter 4

ON THE CHURCH OF LANFRANC

THE HISTORY OF THE CHURCH of Lanfranc has been given at length in the latter part of the first chapter, from which it appears that that archbishop erected it complete and new from the foundations in seven years (Art. 17), and furnished it with the necessary ornaments. And for no reason recorded, it appears that at the suggestion and with the assistance of his successor Anselm, the priors and monks of the monastery took down the east end or choir within the twenty years after its completion, and erected it on an increased scale (Art. 22). Now although Prior Ernulf appears to have had the greatest share in the masonry of the building, yet his successor Conrad completed the decoration of this choir so admirably that Gervase calls it by his name. As no ruin, fire, or other casualty has been recorded, it must be assumed that the sole reason for this change was that the monks did not think their church large enough for the importance of their monastery; and above all, that they wanted shrine room for the display of the relics which our first chapter has shewn them so assiduously collecting and so devoutly venerating, according to the fashion of their times; and also for the proper disposition of their ancient archbishops, most of whom appear to have been canonized.

And as it will presently appear that the area of this church was nearly doubled by the alteration, the necessity of enlargement must have been sufficiently predominant in their minds to account for the taking down of the old choir, without its being necessary to seek for additional reasons by supposing that fires or failures of the structure compelled the change.

Gervase has given us a complete and detailed account of the parts of Lanfranc's church that remained in his time (Chap. 3, Art. 3), that is, the nave, central tower, western towers, transepts and their eastern chapels; the choir or eastern arm of its cruciform plan only being deficient. And of this and of the arrangement of the choir in that state of the building, he confesses himself to be wholly ignorant. In the existing building it happens that the nave and transepts have been transformed into the Perpendicular style of the fourteenth century, and the central tower carried up to about double its original altitude in the same style. Nevertheless several indications may be detected, which shew that these changed parts stand upon the old foundations of Lanfranc. The north-western tower of the nave indeed (B, fig. 3) was only taken down in 1834, and drawings of it are preserved in some of the modern descriptions of the cathedral. It was 113 feet high, and divided by tablets into five stories, of which the lower was plain and 50 feet in height, the next 23 feet with a single window, and the remaining three still less and less, and decorated with arcade-work, which is well represented in Mr. Britton's engravings.[y] The Norman plinth still remains within the nave on each side of the side aisles, from which we learn that the total breadth of Lanfranc's nave was 72 feet. Portions of Norman ashlaring about the transepts (as, for example, at their extreme eastern angles at I and P, fig. 5. and elsewhere, as shewn by the different tints) shew that the transepts also are on the original foundations. The outside of the west wall over the cloister door G also retains Norman ashlaring and the trace of the original clerestory windows.[z] The eastern piers of the great tower still shew Norman ashlaring on their eastern faces, and there can be little doubt that the Norman nucleus still remains within the western piers also of the same tower.

Now Lanfranc, before he was made archbishop of Canterbury, was the first abbot of the monastery of St. Stephen at Caen, the

y Elevation. Britton, pl. 3. View, pl. 6. Britton.
z This is shewn in pl. 4. Britton.

church of which was built under his direction, begun in 1064, and dedicated in 1077, after his appointment to Canterbury. The two churches were therefore in building at the same time. The church at Caen, like that of Canterbury, has had its original choir replaced by one in the style of the thirteenth century, probably for a similar reason, enlargement. The portions which it retains are alike in plan and arrangement to the corresponding parts of Canterbury; alike in the number of piers, in having western towers, transepts without aisles, a central tower, eastern chapels to the transepts, and the pillar and vault at the end of each transept. Nay, even in dimensions, they are, with slight differences, the same. The breadth between the walls of the nave of St. Stephen's[a] is 73 feet, which is one foot greater than at Canterbury. The length from the west end to the tower space is 187 feet, the same as at Canterbury. The extreme length of the transept is 127 feet; also that of Canterbury, as nearly as it can now be ascertained. The width of the central alleys was apparently less at Canterbury than at Caen, and so also were the altitudes. It will presently appear that the ceiling of Canterbury was about 63 feet from the pavement, whilst that of Caen was about 70 feet. This can be ascertained in the former case from the heads of the original clerestory windows that remain. We cannot now tell whether this singular, and I believe hitherto unnoticed, resemblance between the two churches extended also to the elevations, for no fragment remains of Canterbury from which to judge, except the western tower, which is not the same in decoration. But as western towers were the last things finished, deviation might have occurred here, although the rest was the same.

In St. Stephen's there is a range of arches above the pier-arches of the nave, which occupy the triforium space, but were originally open to the side-aisles, the present vault being a manifest insertion of a later period. Now this peculiarity also occurs in the nave of Rochester, which perhaps derived it from its neighbour Canterbury.

a The dimensions and plan of St. Stephen's, at Caen, are derived from Mr. Pugin's *Normandy*.

The extent of Lanfranc's choir can only be surmised from other examples and analogies. The plan, fig. 3 (p. 38), shews the church immediately before the fire, in accordance with Gervase's descriptions and existing remains, as will be presently explained. In this plan I have distinguished the parts which I conceive to be Anselm's work by a different tint of shading.

The mid alley of this choir is eight feet wider than the nave, and between the extreme walls there is a difference of thirteen feet in the average. But we may be sure that the original choir of Lanfranc was, in accordance with all examples, either of the same width as the nave or rather less, and it follows therefore that Ernulf must have taken down the old choir as far as the tower piers. Indeed the peculiar form of these eastern piers shews that they were appendages. In the original work as I suppose it to have existed, the arches and wall of the choir, following the line of the nave and tower-arches, would serve as a direct eastern abutment to them; but as the new wall of the choir was thrown four feet on one side of the line of abutment, it became necessary to give greater strength, and thus, as I suppose, the projecting wall with its semi-pillar W was introduced and made to slope, as shewn in the plan, so as to lay as much hold as possible upon the tower pier. The form of this pier is shewn in detail in fig. 13[b] (See page 77).

The breadth of Lanfranc's choir being thus supposed to be the same as that of the nave, the length and number of its pier-arches may be surmised from cotemporary examples. St. Stephen's at Caen has lost its old choir, but its enlarged choir has four pier-arches on each side. Its cotemporary church of the Holy Trinity at Caen has two pier-arches. So also St. George de Boscherville. In our English

b In this plan the pier of Lanfranc is of course inserted from conjecture. The moldings of the fourteenth century, which clothe its northern and western parts, will be referred to in a subsequent chapter. The small portion of ashlaring which still remains at D, separated by seams from the masonry both of Ernulf and from that of the fourteenth century, is probably part of the original pier. D C is the face of the original pier-arches of Lanfranc, A B that of the present ones; a b c is the plan of the pier in the crypt below.

examples the number of pier-arches is generally four, but several cases occur of two and of three. Bury had five, but this was very unusual.[c]

We can only account for the impatient destruction of Lanfranc's choir by supposing that it had the smallest number, namely two, for if it had had four they would scarcely have been pulled down, but would have remained, and had the increased length and eastern transepts added to them. And as the object of this archbishop was to complete his monastery, and introduce a new and more rigid

[c]

	No. of arches	Date of foundation	Extreme width interior
Gloucester	3	1079	84
Winchester	4	1079	83
Hereford	3	…	73
St. Albans	2	…	76
Rochester	4	…	65
Bury	5	…	68
Ely	4	…	71
Worcester	2	1084	72
Evesham	4	…	70
Durham	4	1093	78
Norwich	4	1096	72
Tewkesbury	2	…	71
Chichester	3	…	60
Petersborough	4	1118	80

These are the only examples I can find in which the date remains, and in which the original number of pier-arches of the choir can be ascertained. The dates are only added when that of the foundation is known. The others are inserted in their probable order, it only being recorded of them that they were built in the life of a given man.

Out of the fourteen examples
seven have four pier-arches
three ... three ... ...
three ... two ... ...
one ... five ... ...

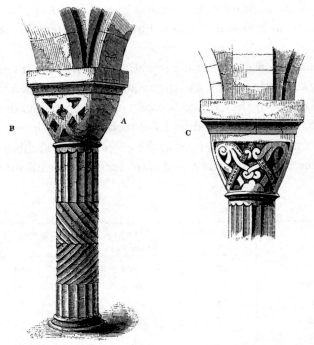

Fig. 12 Column in crypt, south-west side with capital of same.

discipline therein, it may easily be supposed that he would erect his church on a moderate scale. Indeed he seems to have copied his own church of Caen with even slightly reduced dimensions, and as the other churches of Normandy were provided with short choirs of two pier-arches, he only thus followed the ordinary examples of his period and country.

But when the spirit of emulation in England led the church build-ers to increase the number of the pier-arches in their choirs, it may well be imagined that the same spirit would induce the monks of the metropolitan church to contemn their own small eastern work, and to commence another with abundance of altar room and chapels, and altogether on an enlarged scale of dimensions. The transverse dimensions given in the note will confirm the same view, for while the original width of the church fell considerably below the average, the new width of the eastern end was equalled only by Gloucester.

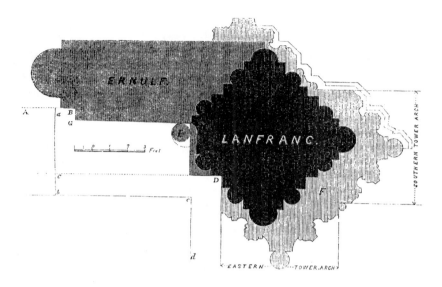

Fig. 13 Plan of the south-eastern pier of the tower.

The shaded parts in a light tint marked *V* in fig. 3. are the con-jectural outline of Lanfranc's eastern end in accordance with the above views, and it will be conceded that men who were about to erect so magnificent an addition to the old church would scarcely hesitate about taking down so small a portion of it.

If this be a correct plan, however, it will follow that no part of the present crypt can belong to Lanfranc's church, unless, indeed, some of its columns may have been used. But in that case they do not stand in their old positions.

In the crypt of the Trinity church at Caen, the shafts stand much nearer together than in that of Canterbury. The former is consider-ably narrower than the latter, yet the shafts stand in four ranks in the first and in two only in the bolder structure of the second; thus the first, notwithstanding that it occupies only one compartment of the choir, together with the apse, has sixteen shafts; while the crypt of Canterbury, which extends under choir and presbytery, through a length of an hundred and sixty-three feet, has only twenty-two shafts. It is not impossible, therefore, that the whole of these shafts may have been taken from the older crypt. However, I have not been able to discover any difference in style or workmanship between these shafts and capitals or their moldings, and the work of Ernulf above. But as the interval of time between the two works was small, and they are both of the same school, perhaps no great difference was to be expected.

The capitals of the columns of the crypt are either plain blocks or sculptured with Norman enrichments. Some of them, however, are in an unfinished state. Figure 12 represents one of the columns with the different sides of its capital.

Of the four sides of the block two are quite plain, as at *A*. One (as *B*) has the ornament roughed out, or 'bosted' as the workmen call it, that is, the pattern has been traced upon the block, and the spaces between the figures roughly sunk down with square edges preparatory to the completion. On the fourth side, as at *C*, the pattern is quite finished. This proves that the carving was executed after the stones were set in their places, and probably the whole of these capitals would eventually have been so ornamented had not the fire and its results brought in a new school of carving in the rich foliated capitals, which caused this merely superficial method of decoration to be neglected and abandoned. In the same way some of the shafts are roughly fluted in various fashions. The figure shews one of them, and the plain ones would probably have all gradually had the same ornament given to them, had not the same reasons interfered.

The word choir is liable to ambiguity, for it is employed in two senses. The primary and proper sense is for the place appropriated to the singers, and hence it is called the 'choir of the singers,' or the 'choir of the monks'.[d] But on the other hand, the word is also employed for the eastern arm of the cross in a church; although the choir of the singers is by no means confined to this part, but often extends into the space under the tower, and even occupies some part

d 'Chorus cantorum,' Edmer, p. 11 above; 'Chorus monachorum,' Gervase, p. 47 above.

of the nave, as we have already seen in the Saxon church. Gervase uses the word in both these senses. In his description of the choir of Conrad it is employed in the first sense, and contrasted with the presbytery. But in the latter part of his work he clearly uses it in the second sense, for in enumerating the number of pillars in the choir, he includes those that belong not merely to the presbytery, but even those of the Trinity chapel.

In attempting to discover the extent of Lanfranc's choir above, I have employed the word in its second sense. But his proper choir 'of the monks,' with so short an eastern portion, probably extended not only under the tower as at Hereford, and of old at Rochester, but even into one or more compartments of the nave, as now at Norwich, Gloucester, Winchester, Chichester, and St. Alban's,[e] and formerly at Ely, Worcester, and Peterborough, while the crypt was confined to the presbytery, for the crypts never extended under the central towers.[f]

The statutes of Lanfranc were addressed to the entire Benedictine order in England, but he evidently had the arrangements of his own church and monastery in view throughout as a model. Amongst the duties of the 'circa' or monastic watchman, he is directed to go round to all the altars in the crypts, and also to those which are beneath on either side of the choir, lest any brother might be sleeping there or otherwise reposing himself unduly.[g] Here not

e The plans in the *Monasticon* and in Willis's *Cathedrals* preserve the original arrangements.

f The English eastern crypts are Canterbury, Winchester, Gloucester, Rochester, Worcester, all founded before 1085. After this they were discontinued except as a continuation of former ones, as in Canterbury and Rochester. The early English crypt of the Lady chapel at Hereford is an exception.

g 'Circumitores monasterii, quos alio nomine *Circas* vocant, juxta Sancti Benedicti præceptum certis horis circumire debent monasterii officinas, observantes incurias, et negligentias fratrum… Completis tribus orationibus quas conventus facit ante Psalmos, quos ante nocturna dicere solet, tunc enim, accensa candela in absconsa, unus eorum in dormitorio debet circumire lectos omnium, et omnia sedilia in necessariis sollicite considerans, ne forte aliquis frater dormiens ibi remanserit, dehinc revertatur in monasterium et circumeat omnia altaria in criptis, et quæ ex utraque parte chori subtus sunt, cooteraque monasterii loca, ubi suspicio poterit esse diligenter observans, ne aliquis frater ibi dormiat, vel jaceat, vel inordinate sedeat.' Statuta Lanfranci, cap. 4; Reyner, p. 235, or Wilkins' *Concilia*, tom. i.

only the crypt and its altars are mentioned, but also the altars at *M* and *H* (fig. 3), which Gervase has explained to have other altars in an upper floor above them. And as I have just shewn that the choir occupied the tower space, these altars are well described in the statute as being on each side of the choir.

Edmer has told us (Chap. 1, Art. 20) that Lanfranc placed the coffins of Bregwin and the other Saxon archbishops upon a vault in the north part of the church, where there was also an altar. This was plainly the vault in the north transept, which was afterwards removed to clear the altar of the martyrdom. This also was the chapel that formed the favourite resort of the Teutonic monk Lambert (Art. 25). Also the 'lofty place outside the choir' where the relics of St. Wilfrid reposed behind an altar, and whence the interior of the choir and persons officiating therein could be seen (Art. 21), was either this north vault or the south vault opposite. This throws some light upon the use of these vaults, namely, for the construction of chapels of peculiar sanctity and privacy, as well as to increase the accommodation for shrines and altars. But after the enlargement of the church, it was thought necessary to adopt a more secure method of depositing these relics (Art. 19, 25), and they were entombed in the places indicated by the figures in plan No.3. And our author's history of this removal is confirmed by the fact, that all the Saxon archbishops are buried in Ernulf's part of the church, with the exception of Fleolgild, Chelnoth, Adhelm, Wolfelm, and Egelnoth. As the pavement of the upper part of the church where these bodies were deposited rests upon the vault of the crypt, and not on the ground, interment was impossible; coffins could only be sunk very slightly at least, if at all, into the spandrels of the vaults. Each must have had a raised tomb sufficiently high to cover them, and this seems to have been of stone, at least in the cases of Dunstan, Odo, Wilfrid, and Theobald. All these tombs have unfortunately disappeared.

Chapter 5

IT MUST BE REMEMBERED, that we have the somewhat intricate task before us of developing three states of the eastern portion of our building. The first as it was left complete by Lanfranc; the second as it was altered and enlarged by Anselm and his priors, in which second state it was attacked by the fire of 1174; the third, as it came out of the hands of the two Williams, after the repairs consequent on the said fire, and in which it remains substantially to this day. In the last chapter I have endeavoured to explain its first state, and now I shall proceed to separate the third state from the second.

Much of the preceding chapter has necessarily been founded upon conjecture and analogy, but the history has now come down to a period of greater certainty. And we may examine the existing building to the east of the great tower in order to discover, by the help of Gervase, which part of it belongs to the period before the fire, and which to the subsequent period.

The western crypt can present no difficulty, even if the style of architecture did not decide the question, for the total absence of any allusion to the rebuilding or repair of this essential part of the structure, must convince us that it was undamaged by the fire and left undisturbed in the subsequent operations, with the sole exception that openings (at *i*, fig. 5) were carefully made to communicate, as Gervase says, between the new crypt and *the old one,* the latter phrase shewing plainly that the old one remained entire. In the plan, fig. 5, I have inserted in the upper half the plan of the crypt in a lighter tint by way of illustrating

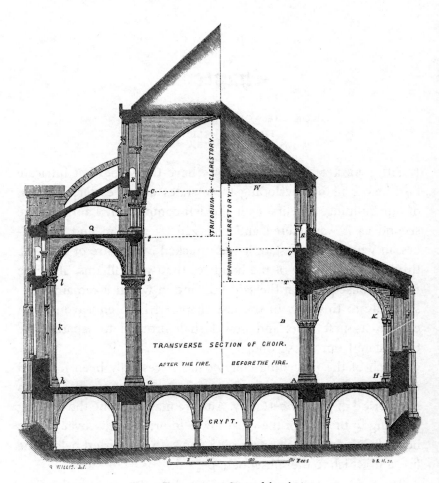

Fig. 14 Transverse section of the choir.

the changes that were made. For the plan of the crypt is very nearly the plan of Ernulf's choir with the exception of the pier

h The present pier *j, k, l, m,* which separates the old crypt from the new, exhibits undisturbed Norman ashlaring on its south side from *j* to *m,* and inserted ashlaring on its north side, as shewn by the different tints in the plan. The south face *k l* receives two arches, one (*k*) is semicircular and is the original arch (*s,* fig. 3.) which Gervase describes (page 50). The other at *l* is one of a pair of pointed arches which rest upon the double shaft marked in the plan, in the middle. The opening *i* which the 'master' so carefully made has its piers on each side clothed with the new masonry. A window probably was originalJy placcd here as it was in the church above.

at *g* and 17, and the small intermediate columns in the
central aisles and transepts.[h]

The crypt of the weſtern
end of the choir being thus
certainly an untouched part
of Ernulf's work, it is equally
certain that the pillars of the
choir, with their pier-arches
and the clereſtory wall above
are as wholly the work of
William of Sens. But with re-
ſpect to the walls of the side
aisles and eaſtern transepts
Gervase is not so explicit,
and requires explanation. It
muſt be remembered that
I am confining myself now
to the parts that lie between
the great tower and the Trinity chapel, for the hiſtory
of every part of the latter is
clear from the foundations
upwards.

Fig. 15 Internal
elevation.

Fig. 16 External
elevation.

To explain the changes which were made in the building by the
works of William, I have drawn, from an accurate examination of
it in its present ſtate, a transverse ſection (fig. 14) and three elevations of compartments (figs 15, 16 and 21); each of these drawings is
separated in the middle by a vertical line, on one side of which the
compartment or ſection appears in its present ſtate, and on the other
in the ſtate before the fire, as far as I have been able to develop it.

'The pillars of the new work were of the same form and diameter
as the old, but were about twelve feet higher.' Now in the north and
south side-aisles at *T W* (plan, fig. 5), which we are told had a plain

83

vault, that is, a waggon vault, a stringcourse may be observed still remaining upon the face of the wall, from which a waggon vault once sprang, and this stringcourse is as nearly as possible twelve feet below the abacus of the opposite columns. With this confirmation of Gervase, the column *A B* (fig. 14) is drawn twelve feet lower than the opposite one *a b,* and of the same diameter. The capital, of course, is sketched in conjecturally. We know that the capitals were 'plain in the old work and sculptured in the new.'[i]

The clerestory windows of the old work still remain in the walls of the eastern transept, although the changes of position from the increased height of the new work have given them the subordinate office of triforium windows. These clerestory windows were of course of the same altitude, and probably of the same form as those of the body of the choir, and I have accordingly inserted them at their proper altitude in fig. 14, and in half elevation at *L,* figs 15 and 16. These two data, namely, the height of the columns and the height and form of the clerestory windows, will enable us to fill up the interior compartment by help of Gervase's description of the choir of 'Conrad' (Page 46).

For 'upon the pillars (*A B,* fig. 15) arches (*B D*) were turned from pillar to pillar.' 'Above these the solid wall (*T C*) was set with small

---

[i] These comparative elevations explain the words of Gervase, when he tells us that the 'new work is higher than the old by so much as the upper windows of the body of the choir as well as of its side-aisles are raised above the marble tabling.' From fig. 16, it appears that the additional altitude given to the walls both of the clerestory and of the side-aisles is as nearly as possible the same as that of each wall above the respective tablings. That is to say, the tabling *d e,* upon which the upper side-windows *G* rest, is nearly at the same altitude as the top of the old wall *e f* under the eaves, and the tabling *h i* under the new clerestory windows *M* is at the same level as the top of the old wall, *i k.*

Most of the crypt windows have been enlarged and provided with late perpendicular tracery, but one or two are left, from which I have inserted the window *E* in these figures. They were 4 ft. wide, 6 ft. 6 in. high, and their sills were level with the top of the abacus and coincident with the earth-table of the wall. They had merely a narrow chamfer on their outer edge. The lights of the old clerestory windows, as preserved in the west wall of the transepts were 4 ft. 10 in. wide, and 7 ft. 9 in. high, and their sills 41 feet from the present pavement of the transept.

and blank windows.'[k] This, in modern nomenclature, was the triforium špace, and it thus clearly appears that there was no gallery in this case, but merely a panelled or arcaded wall, as in the church of the Holy Trinity at Caen. 'Above this wall was the passage which is called triforium (*C*), and the up-

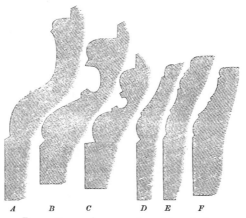

Fig. 17 Bases of peers and vaulting-shafts.

per windows (*L*),' that is, in modern nomenclature, the *clereštory* gallery and its clereštory windows. 'Upon it rešted the roof and a ceiling (*W*, fig. 14), decorated with excellent painting.' 'The proportions of the section, fig. 14, cannot be essentially wrong, and comparing it with the section of the exišting building on its left side, it will appear that the walls and windows of the present side-aisles are of much greater height than the old ones, and that therefore they mušt have been either raised or entirely rebuilt by William.

A close examination to determine this point furnished me with two tešts by which to separate the work of Ernulf from that of William; one in the bases, the other in the masonry.

The bases of the piers and of the vaulting-shafts agaišt the wall of the side-aisles are represented in fig. 17, in which *A* is the base of the semi-pillar of Ernulf's addition to the tower-pier, *B* is the base which is employed for the whole of the remaining pillars of the new choir. *C D E F* are the bases of the shafts of the side-aisle walls.

In these profilcs *A D E F* have rude moldings, which are little

---

k I have rendered here the 'parvulis et obscuris feneštris' small blank windows or panels, for in later times such panels were called *orbs*, blind windows. See 'Nomenclature of the Middle Ages.' The interior elevation of the clereštory and triforium of the old choir in fig. 15 are of course sketched in without authority 'pour fixer les idées,' my purpose being solely to shew the relative elevation of their principal members to those of the present, i. e. of William of Sens' work, rešpectively.

better than scratches upon the surface, and *B C* have well cut mold-ings with a deep undercut hollow, and well-finished fillets. As *A* belongs to the known work of Ernulf, *D E F* may be safely assigned to him, and *C* as securely given to William from its resemblance to the base, *B*, of William's pillars. In the plan, fig. 5, I have distin-guished those portions that have the first bases with a different tint from those that have the second.

The masonry of the vaulting-shafts is also of two kinds, as shewn in fig. 18. One kind, *B*, which always starts from the Ernulf base, is built of small stones, two or three in each course of the cylinder. The other kind, *A*, is generally of higher stones than the former, and always has one stone only in each course of the cylinder. More-over, this latter kind, when it starts from a base, has always the William base, but is also found at the upper part of all the vaultmg-shafts of the side-aisles. Thus in fig. 14. the vaulting-shaft *h, k, l* will either have the Ernulf base and small masonry (as in fig. 19) up to *k*, with large masonry from *k* to *l*, or else it will have the William base combined with the large masonry (as in fig. 20) throughout.[l] The figure (18) was sketched from a shaft of the first kind at the junc-tion *k* of the two. These facts, I think, can leave no doubt that the original vaulting-shafts of the side-aisles were allowed to remain, and were merely lengthened to suit the increased height which the section shews was required, and that in one or two cases, for obvious reasons, the shafts requiring to be shifted in position were rebuilt from the ground, in which case William gave them his own base.

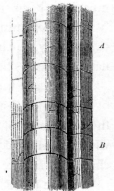

But there is another proof that the present vaulting-shafts are merely adapted from the old ones. Fig. 19 shews the base of one of those vault-

Fig. 18 Two kinds of masonry.

[l] The masonry of the main piers is of the most solid description; the courses of *a b*, fig. 14, are carefully laid down to scale. The shaft of this column is built of seven stones only, 3 ft. 8 in. in diameter, the lowest 4 ft. 2 in. high, and the remainder diminishing; and this is the way in which they are all constructed.

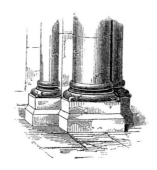

Fig. 19 Ernulf base.   Fig. 20 William base.

ing-shafts that has the Ernulf base and masonry. It consists of a half cylindrical shaft in the centre, which rises, lengthened, as already described, to carry the transverse rib, but at the sides are two bases, which evidently once had small lateral shafts upon them, but which now are left vacant in every instance.

This will be best explained by fig. 21, which is an elevation of one compartment of the side-aisle wall, divided as before to shew the Ernulf design in immediate comparison with that of William.[m] An adjacent compartment (*R S* in the plan, fig. 5) is added in explanation. Now in the original design these lateral shafts find their office in carrying the groins of the vault, and in fact their disposition is exactly that of the side-aisles of Ely nave, a cotemporary work. But in William's design the central shaft (*h l*) carries the transverse rib, and the diagonal ribs are made to spring from the square edges of the pier behind the shaft, by which greater lightness is given, but at the same time the old lateral shafts lose their office, and in fact are removed from the base upwards. In this elevation the masonry is indicated: *h k* is Ernulf's work, and *k l* William's addition. But the angle pier (*M*) has been wholly rebuilt; its base and its masonry are the work of William (fig. 20); and in this instance he has oddly enough introduced a small lateral shaft (*N*) in the very position from which he had removed all the older ones. The forms of the capitals, as at *l*, in all these examples, shew that the removal was

m This elevation is drawn from the north aisle, at *Q R S* on the plan, fig. 5.

87

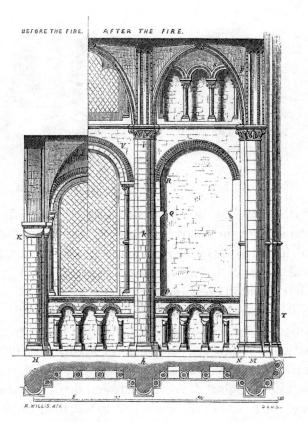

Fig. 21 Elevation of one compartment, north aisle.

coeval with the original alteration, for they contain no provision for receiving these lateral shafts.

The same test of the bases, combined with the style of decoration, proves that the arcade at the base of this wall, and the piers of the windows, are also the work of Ernulf. Now it will be remembered that twelve feet were added to the height of this wall. Several indications shew that the windows, although retaining their piers, and even their arch heads, have yet been raised about three feet eight inches, by the addition of that quantity to their piers, and the resetting of their arch heads. One of these indications is preserved in the compartment *h N* (fig. 21). This is the side of a staircase-tower, as shewn in the plan (*R S*, fig. 5); and accordingly, instead of a window, we find here only a blank panel, bounded by an arch of a similar form. But the original imposts of this arch remain at Q, and its jambs have been raised from Q to R.[n]

The windows being raised so much less than the wall, a space above them still remained to be decorated, and this is occupied by a gallery, or 'triforium' (P, fig. 14), with an arcade and window, which is clearly shewn in these drawings; and the reason for its introduction as clearly explained by comparing the old disposition with the new. The section fig. 14 also shews the difference of the triforia in the two states of the building as contrasted by Gervase. 'There (in the old work) was a single triforium (N), but here (in the new work) are two in the choir (Q and R) and a third (P) in the aisle of the church' (Page 60).

But to return to the plan, fig. 5. By comparing the position of the pillars in this plan (and in the section fig. 6) with the piers of the crypt below, it will be remarked that they do not all stand one over the other. Taking them in order from the tower, I. is the original semi-cylinder with the Ernulf base; the remainder have William's base, and II stands upon the crypt wall; III and IV near the western edges of the respective piers below; V hangs half over it, and VI has its centre beyond the edge. This pier of the crypt has been fortified to bear this unequal pressure, by the addition of a half octagon pier, having William's moldings, and represented in the next figure.[o]

The next pier of the crypt has no corresponding pillar above it, although in the original choir of Ernulf there was one, for the series of pier-arches was in that building carried uninterruptedly across

[n] Whether the whole of the windows were raised by exactly the same amount may fairly be doubted. For example, in Anselm's chapel the west window (r in the plan, fig. 5) is a lofty and narrow Norman window, with shafts and moldings like those described in the text. Its inner opening is 16 ft. 8 in. high, and 4 ft. 4 in. broad. But there are unequivocal remains of the original springing of the arch from the jambs, which shew that its height was at first only 9 ft. 9 in., so that this window has been raised about seven feet, unless indeed, this arch was a kind of transom.

[o] The places of these piers in the plan, as well as of the side aisle vaulting-shafts, are laid down from measures which I took myself, with the express view of determining their relative positions.

Fig. 22 Half octagon pier in the crypt.

the transepts, as at Strasburg, Pisa, and several other foreign cathedrals.[p] VII stands a little to the east of the centre of its crypt pier, but does not hang over it. VIII would have hung over had it not been that the corresponding pier of the crypt is here considerably broader than the rest, from which it may be inferred that in Ernulf's choir the pillar in this place was larger than the others, and probably of a compound form, by way of separating the pillars of the eastern circuit from those of the straight rank. IX stands also near the edge of Its crypt pier. But now the difference of plan in the two churches begins to shew itself, for the crypt piers follow the circuit of the apse, but the line of pillars above is only slightly deflected to avoid the towers, as Gervase has so minutely explained. X is thus thrown far from any of the crypt piers below, and accordingly we here find a pillar erected in the aisle of the crypt immediately below it, as shewn in the following figure.

p See p. 47–48 and 66 above. 'There a wall set upon pillars divided the crosses from the choir,' &c.

Fig.23 Pillar erected in the aisle of the crypt.

XI stands on the east wall of Ernulf's crypt, and the remaining pillars were erected by the same architect as the piers of the crypt below them, and consequently the one stands immediately over the other throughout.

The reasons for this variation in the spacing of the piers are to be found in the crypt. The arches of the crypt and the vaults of its side aisle are arranged in an equally spaced series across the entrance of the transept. But the transept of the crypt is wider than the two severeys of the side-aisle that are in contact with it, and thus its west wall *ef* is set a little farther westward than the face of the arch of the crypt that springs from *S* to VI, and the wall above the eastern arches of the apse a little farther eastward than the arch that springs from *T* to VII.

In the choir of Ernulf the transepts were cut off from the body by the continuity of the pier-arches and the wall above, and each transept was therefore a separate room with a flat ceiling. The wall that came off northward from the piers VI and VII respectively must

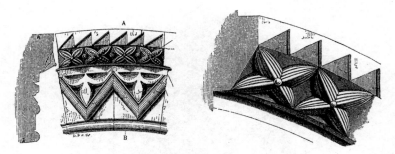

Fig. 25 Dog-tooth moldings.

have fallen back after passing the single piers *S* and *T*, so that each transept was about two feet narrower in the compartment next to the body of the choir than it was at its extreme gables (plan fig. 3). But in the new design of William the transepts were opened to the central portion, and the triforium and clerestory of the choir were turned at right angles to their courses at the piers VI and VII and thus formed the side-walls of the transepts. Therefore these piers (the principal piers, as Gervase calls them) were set farther asunder, the one to the west, the other to the east, so that the transept might have the same breadth next to the pier-arches as at its farthest extremity. And thus the piers of the choir were thrown out of coincidence with those of the crypt below.

The angle piers at *S* and *T* above have been rebuilt from the base upwards, and have William's base and large stonemasonry throughout. This seems to confirm the above explanation, by shewing that the form and projection of the original pier made it necessary to take it entirely down.

But the entire interior of the eastern transept has been most skilfully converted from Ernulfian architecture to Willelmian,[q] (if I may be allowed the phrase for the nonce). The contrast between them is shewn by the sketch fig. 24, taken in the side-aisles of the choir

---

[q] In the south aisle of the choir it happens that one of Ernulf's arches has been taken out, and one of William's substituted, exactly like those in the transepts, whether as the beginning of a plan for an entire change, or whether as a repair I know not; but the juxtaposition of the two affords an excellent comparison. Vide fig. 8, p. 65 above.

from the pier VII and shewing the pier *S* in the middle, having the wall on one side running down the side-aisle, with Ernulf's arcade below, and on the other side (in the transept) having the pointed arcade with William's base and moldings, and the characteristic Early English dog-tooth.[r] There are several reasons which made it necessary thus completely to transform the transepts, although the side-aisle walls were merely raised. First, the side-aisles were completely protected by their vaults from the burning and falling timbers of the roof, and thus their stone-work and ornaments would escape the scathing and bruises which would necessarily attack the walls of the transepts. Thus the Ernulfian arcades of the latter probably suffered so much as not to be worth preserving.

Again, it was necessary that the triforium and clerestory of the new design should be carried along the walls of these transepts, which were before the fire probably ornamented by a continuation of those of Ernulf. But figs 14 and 15 will shew that the respective levels of these essential members were so different in the old and new works that the only parts of them that could be retained were the windows of the old clerestory, which falls just above the new triforium tablet, and accordingly these old windows may still be seen in the triforia of the transepts, surmounted by the new pointed

---

[r] Although the ornament known by the name of the dog-tooth was retained as a characteristic and most usual embellishment of the Early English style, yet it was adopted some time previous to the complete formation of that style. In Canterbury I found the specimen represented in fig. 25 in the arches of the small circular building commonly termed the Baptistery, and which now contains the modern font in its upper story. But I have ascertained that this building forms part of the curious hydraulic system by which the monastery was anciently supplied with water. The whole was the work of Prior Wibertus, who died in 1167; he succeeded Prior Walter, who took office in 1153, but the time of whose death is uncertain. Wibert however was previously sub-prior. In a long list of his works the following occurs. 'Aqueductum cum stagnis et lavatoriis et piscinis suis; quam aquam fere milliario ab urbe intra Curiam et sic per omnes ipsius Curie officinas mirabiliter transduxit.' Cotto MS. Claud., c. 6. fol. 166. Ang. Sac., tom. i. p. 138. This system I hope to explain at length in another place, but from the date which it assigns to this early specimen of the dog-tooth, I have departed in this instance from the rule which I have laid down of confining myself in this work to the Cathedral, without attempting to describe the buildings about it, which are of sufficient number and importance to be reserved for a separate investigation.

Fig. 26 An elegant pier base.

clerestory windows. But the whole of the arcade-work and moldings in the interior of these transepts belongs to William of Sens, with the sole exception of the lower windows, which have been adapted and treated as those of the side-aisles already described.[s] Even the arches which open from the east wall of these transepts to the apses have been changed for pointed arches, the piers of which have the singularly elegant base here represented.

And as these arches were originally of the same height as the pier-arches, and on account of the apse behind them did not admit of being raised twelve feet like those pier-arches, the space thus left between them and the new triforium tablet is occupied by a blank arcade of pointed arches, which seems to have been suggested by the similar blank arcade of the Ernulfian triforium, the level of which it very nearly occupies. This blank arcade is also continued on the other walls of the transept over the lower windows.

Leaving the transepts we come to the eastern side-aisles, and here we find the Ernulfian arcade remaining below, but all the vaulting-shafts T, U, V (plan, fig. 5), inserted with William's base. It is probable, that as according to Gervase, p. 59, a waggon vault was originally employed in this place, the vaulting-shafts were either entirely omitted or merely carried transverse ribs.[t] It will be seen that the places of the

---

[s] Britton's plate v. is a good section and elevation of the eastern transepts; the elevation shews the exterior wall, with the Ernulfian arcade, lower window and clerestory window (now the triforium window), all round-headed. The pointed clerestory window of William surmounts the whole. The section which shews the eastern wall of the transept exhibits the interior lining, wholly of William's architecture as above explained, and the roundheaded windows of Ernulf are seen behind. The pointed arches inserted in front of the apses are also shewn on a larger scale in Britton's plate xix, and in fig. 12. pl. xviii of the *Companion to the Glossary*.

new ones do not coincide with the shafts in the crypt below, and yet are strangely placed out of agreement with the opposite piers VII, VIII, IX; in fact, four vaulting-shafts stand opposite to three piers, and the vaulting-ribs are carried awkwardly across in the manner shewn by the dotted lines on the lower half of the plan. This number of vaulting-shafts is intended to accommodate the ancient window *s*, which, as Gervase has recorded, stood opposite to the high Altar. The base repre-sented in the annexed figure occurs in this aisle on the north side.

Fig. 27 Base of vaulting shaft.

We have now arrived at the towers of St. Andrew and St. Anselm. The projecting angle *o*, from which the curvature of the apse wall originally sprang, is ingeniously rounded off and ornamented by three shafts and some arcade-work. But in Anselm's tower the arch of communication 28, is a round arch,[u] at first sight plainly of the Ernulfian period, having plaited-work capitals and moldings with shallow hollows. A similar arch opens at *p q* on the eastern side of the tower into its apse.

But a closer examination will shew that both these arches have undergone alteration. Fig. 28 is the profile of the first on the side next to the choir. The molding on the edge *A* is the same as that of the pier-arches of William's choir throughout, and has the billet like them, as well as a more deeply sunk hollow, and more members than the edge-mold at *B*, which is the usual Norman one. On the chapel side of this arch the moldings are like these from *C* to *B*, but instead of the greatly projecting arch *A*, there are three broad fasciæ of small projection, the uppermost of which has Ernulf's notched ornament shewn in fig. 31 (p. 99).

---

t A vaulting cell must have been introduced transversely to this waggon vault from each pier-arch, and also from the window *s* and the arch 28 respectively.

u Britton, pl. ix.

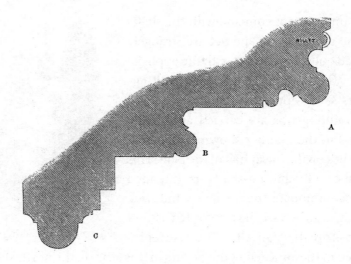

Fig. 28 Section of arch leading to Anselm's chapel.

I am inclined to believe that both these arches were reset and re-duced in span after the fire, probably to increase their strength and that of their piers, on account of the loss of abutment at *o*, when the circular wall of the choir-apse was removed. This operation has evi-dently been performed upon the apsidal arch *p q*, the moldings of which are the same as those on the chapel side of the other arch. But in the apsidal arch, the original capital for the fasciæ above described is now to be seen half buried in the wall, and has another inserted in front of it in such a manner as plainly to shew that the whole pier is in advance of its original position and that the arch above has conse-quently been reduced in span, although the original voussoirs and capitals have been reset. There are also indications of change in the abacus molds.

The apse piers retain their original bases, but the bases of the arch 28 have been cut away to make room for Archbishop Mepham's monumental screen which now occupies this place. The opposite or north tower of St. Andrew is now closed up and occupied by a floor and other insertions that prevented me from examining the state of its arches.

I shall now make a few remarks upon the comparative styles of architecture of the building in its two states.

Gervase points out the following differences between the works before and after the fire. The elongation of the pillars by twelve feet, retaining the same diameter, from which it follows that they were converted from a height of four diameters to one of seven. The old capitals were plain, the new ones most artistically sculptured. The old arches and every thing else either plain, or sculptured with an axe and not with a chisel, but in the new work first-rate sculpture abounded every where. In the old work no marble shafts, in the new innumerable ones. Plain vaults instead of ribbed behind the choir.

In the few portions that remain of the works of Ernulf the mold-ings are simple and shallow, as already shewn in the bases (fig. 17, page 85), and the decoration consists of a peculiar and shallow class of notched ornament, of which many examples exist in other buildings of the period. One case has already been figured in page 65, where an arch of the in-terior arcade of the side-aisle walls is shewn in contrast with an arch of William's work. In the decoration of these arch-es of Ernulf no moldings are employed, but a kind of dou-ble zigzag is used, which is repeated on a smaller scale upon the face of the tablet above, and these zigzags are brought out by simply cut-ting two very slightly inclined facets between the points, in a manner that is very clearly shewn in the figure. The stair-case towers at the western

Fig. 29 Norman arches, north side, exterior.

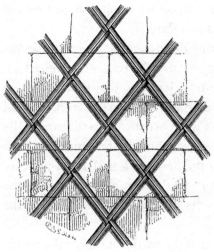

Fig. 30 Diaper work in passage to crypt.

side of the transepts contain very beautiful ſpecimens of this decoration of Ernulf.[x]

Figure 29 is a portion of an arcade, which is continued as a belt of decoration on the outside of all that portion of Ernulf's wall which remains. It correſponds in position to the arcade already described within, and may be considered a very fair ſpecimen of the ſtyle of decoration of our architect. And it is remarkably identified with him by the occurrence of an arcade almoſt the same[y] as this againſt the interior wall of the eaſt end of the chapter-house at Rocheſter, which is the recorded work of this Ernulf, after he became bishop of Rocheſter (Art. 23, Ch. 1 above). Another similar coincidence of ornament is to be found in a very singular diaper represented in the figure. This decorates the walls on the south side of the passage to the crypt from the martyrdom transept; and also the front of the chapter-house of Rocheſter.

In figure 29 the small arches have the usual Norman edge-mold, a shallow hollow and round; and the interſecting arches have a billeted round and the same shallow notched double zigzag as the interior arcade of fig. 11. The abacus-mold is the same as that within (see fig. 41, p. 103), and the capitals are some of them left plain (as all the interior arcade capitals that remain are); but others have the characteriſtic grotesque and plaited decoration of the time, very different from the rich foliated and artiſtic capital of the French architect. Specimens of the same kind of Norman capital occur in the crypt (fig. 12, p. 76), and may also be seen in the entrance and apsidal arch of Anselm's chapel.

[x] Britton, pl. v and xxii (miscalled Anselm's tower).
[y] This arcade is now seen at the foot of the ſtaircase of the Dean's house at Rocheſter, which occupies the site of the eaſt end of the chapter-house.

The following figures are well adapted to place in contrast the two styles of workmanship of the artists in question, Ernulf and William, for they are found in juxtaposition, and the second seems designed to imitate the first, or at least to harmonize with it.

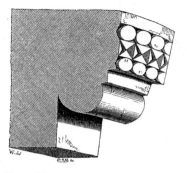
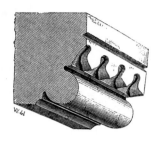

Fig. 31 Norman window heads.   Fig. 32 Arches in side aisle of choirs.

These occur in the walls of the side-aisles of the interior. Fig. 31 is the ornament of all the window-heads, and belongs to Ernulf. Fig. 32 is the ornament of the arch against the wall of the additional work above, which was raised by William of Sens (for example, it occurs behind the spandrel F, fig. 21, although concealed by it in the figure).

Now each of these figures consists of a bold round or bow-tell, having above it a broad face, which is ornamented by sculpture. But the sculpture in the first is worked out by shallow notches as already explained, while in the second it is deeply cut into a graceful series of leaves. Also the edge below the bowtell is left square in the first example, but in the second has a small well-wrought hollow. And in all respects the second example shews the employment of more effective tools, as well as an improved taste. It is, to borrow the words of our author, wrought with a chisel instead of being hewed out with an axe. It must be observed, however, that the axe is not quite so rude a weapon in the hands of a mason as it might appear at first sight. The French masons use it to the present day with great dexterity in carving.

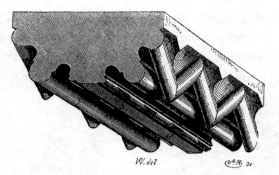

Fig. 33 Transverse rib-mold of side aisle.

The moldings of William of Sens exhibit much variety, but are most remarkable for the profusion of billet-work, zigzag and dog-tooth, that are lavished upon them. The richest mold is perhaps that of the transverse ribs of the side-aisle vaults, of which a fragment is shewn in figure 33. This is employed throughout the side-aisles not only of the choir, but also of Trinity chapel as well as in the pier-arches of the corona.

The moldings of the other vault-ribs will be sufficiently understood by the sections in the following page.

A is the diagonal rib of the side-aisles of the choir; B the diagonal rib of the central vaults, which differs from the latter only in its greater breadth, and in the introduction of a fillet below, by which that increased breadth is obtained without altering the profile at the sides; *C* is the transverse rib of the central vaults. And it will be seen that the diagonal ribs have the dog-tooth ornament, while the billet is given to the transverse ribs. The rib *A* is also employed for the low vault (*P*, fig. 6) under the patriarchal chair. This vault, therefore, is shewn to be the work of one of the Williams, and not to be part of the ancient arrangements of Ernulf. The pier-arch mold is shewn in fig. 37, and that of the triforium in fig. 38. These are continued all round Trinity chapel. The pier-arch has the billet mold in its upper order of voussoirs *D*, and the dogtooth in the sub-order *E*. This mixture of two ornaments, one of which is characteristic of the Norman and the other of the Early English,

100

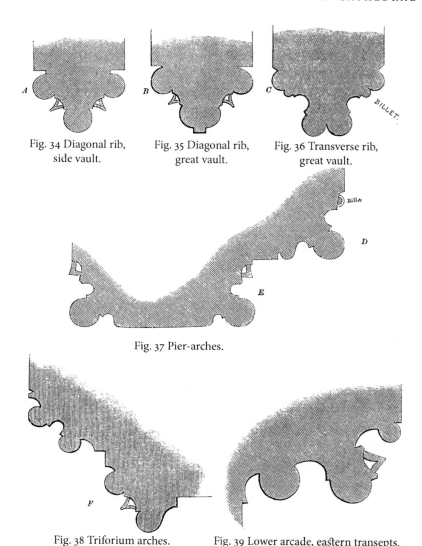

Fig. 34 Diagonal rib, side vault.

Fig. 35 Diagonal rib, great vault.

Fig. 36 Transverse rib, great vault.

Fig. 37 Pier-arches.

Fig. 38 Triforium arches.

Fig. 39 Lower arcade, eastern transepts.

is worth comparing with the mixture of round and pointed arches throughout. The molding *F* is merely half the diagonal rib (fig. *A* above), and is thus employed singly in several other parts of William of Sens' work, as for example, in the upper arcade of fig. 21, at *S*, and for all the small arcades in the transepts, excepting those on the ground, of which one arch has been figured in page 65, and the moldings of it are exhibited in fig. 39.

The general arrangement of the architecture may be seen from the elevations (figs 15 and 16), or in the numerous views that have been published. One of its most curious features is the indiscriminate employment of round or pointed arches, as the case may be. This may have arisen either from the indifference of the architect to this mixture of forms, or else from deliberate contriv-

Fig. 40 Crypt of Trinity chapel.

ance; for as he was compelled, from the nature of his work, to retain round-headed arcades, windows, and arches, in the side-aisles, and yet was accustomed to and desirous of employing pointed arches in his new building, he might discreetly mix some round-headed arches with them, in order to make the contrast less offensive by causing the mixture of forms to pervade the whole composition, as if an intentional principle. In the triforium there are two orders of arches, as shewn in fig. 15 above. The outer arch is a semicircle; the two inner which it circumscribes are pointed. The clerestory arch is pointed. The transverse ribs of the great vault are some pointed and some round; the diagonal ribs all round. The pier-arches all pointed, excepting two in Trinity chapel (see fig. 6). The side-aisle vaults have semicircular ribs. In the triforium of the transepts pointed arches and semicircular are placed side by side.[z]

It is a very difficult task to separate the original work of William the Englishman from that of his predecessor. Gervase, indeed, has told us pretty exactly all that was erected during his superintendence, but much of this must have formed part of the original design of William of Sens. The erection of the new Trinity chapel, or chapel of Becket, which took place wholly under the direction of the Englishman, must have been intended from the beginning; for the contrivance of narrowing the central alley of the choir, for the double purpose of avoiding the old towers and of adjusting the width to agree with that of the ancient chapel of the Trinity, was due to the French artist, seeing that the inclined part of the choir

z Britton, pl. xix.

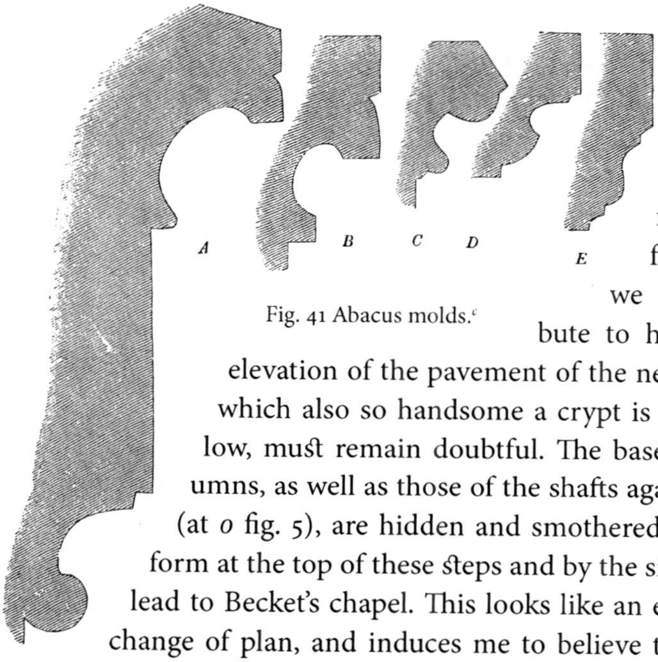

Fig. 41 Abacus molds.[c]

(namely, the piers IX, X, XI) was carried up to the clerestory before his fall. Whether we are to attribute to him the lofty elevation of the pavement of the new chapel, by which also so handsome a crypt is obtained below, must remain doubtful. The bases of his columns, as well as those of the shafts against the wall (at *o* fig. 5), are hidden and smothered by the platform at the top of these steps and by the side steps that lead to Becket's chapel. This looks like an evidence of a change of plan, and induces me to believe that the lofty crypt below may be considered as the unfettered composition of the English architect.[a] Its style and its details are wholly different from those of William of Sens. The work, from its position and office, is of a massive and bold character, but its unusual loftiness prevents it from assuming the character of a crypt, and it is to be regretted that the windows are not opened and glazed, by which its beauties would become more apparent.[b] Two of the pier-arches are semicircular and the others pointed; the only molding on their lower edges is a plain narrow chamfer, and a slight square

a It is probable that in the original plan of the French architect the pavement of the chapel of St. Thomas and the side-aisles were on the same level as those of the choir. This is the most usual disposition of a presbytery of this kind; or the pavement of his chapel might have been raised without raising the side-aisles, as in Edward the Confessor's chapel at Westminster.

b For views and details of this crypt see Britton, pl. xii.; Parker's *Glossary,* vol. iii. plates 5, 28, 29.

c B Trinity chapel; *C* lower arcade, arcade (*S*, fig. 21.) ; *E* Ernulf's lower north-east transept; *D* William's upper arcade (fig. 21).

edge serves to separate the two courses of voussoirs. Fig. 40 is the rib-mold, the capital is shewn at *A*, in fig. 41, and the impost-molds that accompany the latter will serve still further to contrast the different styles.

There is one part of the detail of this crypt which differs especially from the work above. The abacus of each of the piers, as well as that of each central shaft, is round; but in the whole of the choir the abacuses are either square, or square with the corners cut off, and for the diagonal ribs these square abacuses are set angularly.

Now the only exception to this rule is, that the round abacus occurs in the piers of the apsidal chapels (12…16, and 35…38, fig. 5) of the east wall of the transepts, the corresponding cylindrical plinths of which have been figured in page 94. It is true that the Englishman finished the transepts in 1179, immediately after the Frenchman's departure; but the question is, of course, whether this part remained for him to do.

The work of these transepts consisted (1) of re-ashlaring and repairing the walls below; (2) adding the arcades and the triforium; (3) raising the arches of the Norman windows below; (4) inserting the pointed arches of these apses, and giving them a pointed character throughout; (5) erecting the new clerestory, and adding the vault. In a new building the lower part is necessarily erected first, and the works proceed regularly upwards, but in a case of this kind there can be little doubt that the essential part, namely, the raising of the clerestory walls and the erection of the vault would be first done, and then the decoration of the lower part, which consisted merely of a new lining to the old walls, would be proceeded with. But as Gervase has distinctly recorded the vaults of these transepts as the last works of the Frenchman, and the finishings of the transepts as the first works of the Englishman, a very probable case is made out in favour of the introduction of the round abacus by him,[d] inasmuch as this is a new feature in the work, and as such, very likely to have been introduced

d I am not attributing the invention to him, but merely the introduction of it into this building.

Fig. 42 Compartment of the corona.

by a new architect; every where else, however, he has adhered to the square abacus of his predecessor, excepting, as before said, in the crypt, where he had none of the previous work to constrain him.

However, it must be very difficult to judge of the unfettered style even of William of Sens, because in every part of his work the retention of the old Norman portions evidently cramps and governs his composition. In the same way, the Trinity chapel of the Englishman is under the influence of the French work of which it is a continuation, and accordingly the same moldings are employed throughout, and the triforium and clerestory are continued at the same level; but the greater elevation of the pavement wholly alters the proportion of the piers to their arches, and gives a new and original, and at the same time a very elegant character to this part of the church compared with the work of the Frenchman, of which, at first sight, it seems to be a mere continuation.

The triforium also of this Trinity chapel differs from that of the choir, in that its four pointed arches instead of being, like them, included under two circular ones (as in fig. 15), are set in the form of an arcade of four arches, of two orders of moldings each. The moldings are the same as in the choir, but the effect of their arrangement is richer. Also in the clerestory, two windows are placed over each pier-arch, instead of the single window of the choir. The mixture of the two forms of arches is still carried on, for although the semicircular arch is banished from the triforium, it is adopted for the pier-arches, as shewn in the section (fig. 6).

However, in the side-aisles of the Trinity chapel, and in the corona, our English William appears to have freed himself almost as completely from the shackles of imitation, as was possible. In the side-aisles the moldings of the ribs still remain the same, but their management in connection with the side walls, and the combination of their slender shafts with those of the twin lancet windows, here for the first time introduced into the building, is very happy.[e] Slender shafts of marble are employed in profusion by William of

e Well represented in Winkles, pl. vii.

Sens, and Gervase expressly includes them in his list of characteristic novelties. But we here find them either detached from the piers, or combined with them in such a manner as to give a much greater lightness and elegance of effect than in the work of the previous architect. This lightness of style is carried still farther in the corona, where the slender shafts are carried round the walls, and made principal supports to the pier-arches, over which is placed a light triforium and a clerestory; and it must be remarked that all the arches in this part of the building are of a single order of moldings, instead of two orders as in the pier-arches and triforium of the choir. The square abacus, however, is used throughout. Fig. 42 represents one compartment of the corona in which these peculiar arrangements are shewn.

The piers of Trinity chapel are composed each of two columns, set one behind the other. This form is also used in one pair of William of Sens' piers (X, fig. 5), but with the addition in the latter of two marble shafts at the sides.

The cathedral of Sens, which dates from 1143 to 1168,[f] has several peculiarities in common with the work of Canterbury; for example, the double piers in question, the foliated capitals, the square abacus, and that set diagonally when appertaining to the diagonal rib-shafts. Also the rings upon some of the slender shafts, and the same system of vaulting the great vault in 'sexpartite ciboria,' that is, in square compartments, each corresponding to two pier-arches on each side, and each having besides the diagonal ribs, and the transverse ribs that bound it, another intermediate transverse rib, so that six vaultingcells thus meet in the keystone.[g]

The mechanical construction of the clerestory in William of Sens' choir is somewhat singular, and is shewn in the transverse section (fig. 14) The floor of the clerestory gallery R is carried by the

[f] See Chapuy, *Cathedrales Français*. The arches in the nave are all pointed, but in the side-aisles of the choir there are 'some round arches, probably the remains of an earlier edifice.

[g] Hence the term' sexpartite,' given to this class of vaults in the Architectural Notes on German Churches, p.72.

triforium arches, but the thin wall of the clerestory windows rests upon a segmental arch S, which springs from the buttresses, and the crown of this arch is so high, that it rises even above the pavement of the clerestory gallery, leaving a small opening by which persons in the latter gallery can see into the triforium below at Q, and hold communication with persons therein.

I shall conclude this chapter by mentioning two long staircases, one of which is shewn at the west end of the south aisle at O, fig. 5, and there is another in the north aisle corresponding to it. These staircases evidently belonged to Ernulf's building, although the eastern pier that bounds them has William's base, and was erected by him. The southern one now turns to the south, and gives access to a room over the chapel of St. Michael (44). They seem to have been originally open to the side-aisles, and they are constructed upon the foundations of the side walls of Lanfranc's original choir. Perhaps the north one was originally built to give access to the passage constructed round the north transept by which the 'pallia' were to be suspended, as Gervase relates, after the destruction of Lanfranc's vault; and the southern one in imitation of it.

Chapter 6

THE HISTORY OF THE CHOIR FROM THE TWELFTH
CENTURY

PRIOR HENRY DE ESTRIA[h] was elected in 1285, and died in 1331, and according to the obituary adorned the church and monastery with various works; amongst which, 'he decorated the choir of the church with most beautiful stone-work delicately carved'.[i] In his Register, however, there is an inventory of the works that were executed under this prior, in which the same is more specifically described thus:

'Anno 1304 and 5. Reparation of the whole choir with three new doors, a new screen or rood-loft (pulpitum), and the reparation of the chapter-house with two new gables... 839 *l.* 7 *s.* 8 *d.*'[j]

These entries must refer to the beautiful stone enclosure of the choir, the greatest part of which still remains. The three doors are the central or western one, and the north and south doors. The present elaborate western screen, or organ-screen as it is now called, is of a much later period, and a little examination of its central archway will detect the junction of this new work with that under consideration. In fact this archway is considerably higher than that of De Estria, which still remains behind it. The apex of his arch reaches but a little above the capitals of the new arch, and the flat space or tympanum thus left between the two is filled up with perpendicular tracery. As this latter screen, elaborate and

---

h Namely, Eastry, in Kent.

i 'Chorum verò Ecelesiæ pulcherrimo opere lapideo subtiliter inciso decenter adornavit.' (Obit. Cant. in *Ang. Sac.,* tom. i. p. 141.)

j 'Anno M°ccc°. quarto et quinto. Reparatio totius chori cum tribus novis ostiis et novo pulpito et reparatio capituli cum duobus novis gabulis.' MS. Cott. Galba, E. IV. fol. 103. The entire document is printed with some inaccuracies by Dart. App., p. iii.

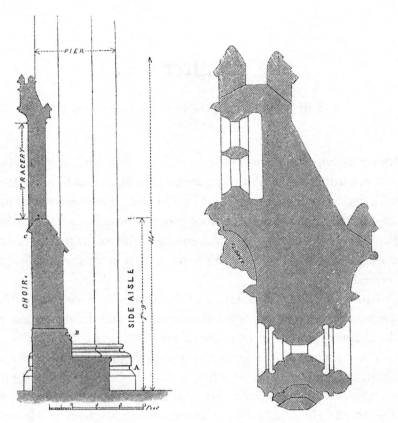

Fig. 43a Section of screen.   Fig. 43b Enlarged section of upper part.

beautiful as it is, has no recorded date, I shall content myself with referring to engravings[k] which sufficiently explain it, and return to the work of De Estria.

The lateral portions of this wall of enclosure are in excellent order. In the western part of the choir, namely, between the eastern transepts and the organ-screen, this wall is built so that its inner face nearly ranges with the inner faces of the pillars; but eastward

k Britton, in pl. xx., has an elevation of the central archway, in which the old arch may be seen under the new one, as above described; also details, in pl. xxi. Wild has a general view in pl. 3.

Fig. 44 North doorway of screen (outer face).

Fig. 45 North doorway and part of screen (inside face).

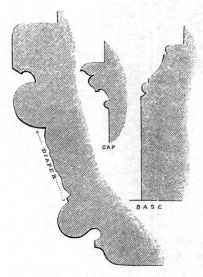

Fig. 46 Moldings of outer face of north doorway of choir.

of the transepts it is built between the pillars. The north doorway remains perfect. The present south doorway, which is in a much later style, is manifestly a subsequent insertion. The construction of this wall of enclosure will be seen from the section (fig. 43), which is drawn from the north-western part of it.[l] It consists of a solid wall, seven feet nine inches in height from the pavement of the side-aisles. It has a stone bench towards the side-aisles, and above that a base, *B*, of the age of William of Sens (*C*, fig. 17 p. 85); so that it is clear that the work of De Estria belongs to the upper part only of the enclosure, which consists of delicate and elaborately worked tracery, surmounted by an embattled crest. The moldings of the crest and of the tracery are shewn more at large in fig. 44. The entire altitude is fourteen feet.

The two annexed views (figs. 44 and 45) represent the inner and outer faces of the north doorway, and shew also a part of the tracery. The moldings of this doorway are given in fig. 46. The singular coincidence of its base-mold with Ernulf's rude base (*D*, fig.17, p. 85) is worth observing. The entire work is particularly valuable on account of its well-established date, combined with its great beauty and singularity.[m]

l In the plinth of the base of the pier, immediately above the chamfered 'ground table,' a square sinking (*A*, fig. 43.) will be seen. This is found in all the piers, and has once received a stout band of iro, which encircled the entire plinth, and the ends of which may still be seen projecting from the masonry of the screen wall.

m A plate, containing an elevation of the tracery of this wall, occurs in Caveler's *Gothic Architecture*. See also Britton, pl. xvii, xxiii. The inserted south door is seen in Wild, pl. 7 and 8.

The shrine of St.Thomas was placed in the centre of the chapel within the enclosure, dotted at 27 in the plan,[n] and had in front of it at *Z* a curious mosaic pavement, which still remains, executed in the manner termed 'Opus Alexandrinum,'[o] in which the pavements of most of the Roman basilicas are wrought, and of which there are also specimens at Westminster abbey in the pavements of the presbytery, of the chapel of Edward the Confessor, and also about his shrine and the tomb of Henry III.

Stow has preserved a description of the shrine of Becket which was demolished in the year 1538.[p] It was built about a man's height all of stone, then upwards of timber plain, within which was a chest of iron containing the bones of Thomas à Becket. The timber-work of this shrine was covered with plates of gold, damasked and em-bossed with wires of gold, garnished with brooches, images, chains, precious stones, and great orient pearls, the spoils of which shrine filled two great chests, one of which six or eight strong men could do no more than convey out of the church; all which was taken to the king's use, and the bones of St. Thomas, by the commandment of the Lord Cromwell, then and there burned to ashes, which was in September in the year 1538, (30 H. VIII).[q] Erasmus supplies the additional information that the golden shrine had a wooden cover suspended by ropes, so that it could be raised easily when the shrine was exhibited. The bones of the saint were not visible, they were de-posited in the upper part of the structure. I may add that there was an altar at the west end of this shrine within the iron rails that sur-rounded it, for in the Statutes of Archbishop Winchelsey[r] there are

n The site of this shrine is marked in Hollar's plan, and moreover the stain of the iron railing which enclosed it, may still be seen in the pavement. ,

o So called from Alexander Severus; see Nibby, *Antichita di Roma* 1830, p. 67.

p A figure of this shrine, given by Dugdale from one of the Cotton manuscripts, has been copied by Battely and others.

q The king's mandate is printed in Wilkins' *Concilia*, vol. iii. p. 836. 'Mandamus ejus ossa ex sepulchro erui et publice comburi,' &c. Dated June 11, 1538. It was carried in to effect on Aug. 19.

r He held the see from A.D. 1294 to 1313. His statutes are ill Wilkins' *Concilia*, vol. ii. p. 244.

express directions for the careful closing of the iron doors before the altar at the head of the feretrum of St. Thomas, namely, the one opposite to the altar as well as that on the north side.⁵ It does not appear how far the other shrines and relics were destroyed at the same time with Becket's, although it can hardly be supposed that Dunstan and Elphege could escape. But in 1541, Archbishop Cranmer seems to have complained to the king how little effect former orders from His

s 'Ostia ferrea ante altare ad capud feretri Sci. Thome vid. tam ex altaris opposito, quam etiam a latere boreali,' &c. The shrine of Edward the Confessor, which still remains, although in a sadly mutilated and neglected state in Westminster abbey, will serve to illustrate the arrangement of Becket's shrine, and probably those of the other principal saints. It stands like Becket's in a chapel separated from the choir and high Altar by a reredos, but yet not a detached building, as the Lady chapels so commonly were. Architecturally speaking, the chapels of Becket and Edward are within the choir at its east end; the pavement in both cases is raised above the level of the choir: and each shrine is a parallelogram on the plan, and stands east and west. The Altar is at its west end, and in contact with it, so that the saint is placed behind the altar 'retro altare,' and reciprocally the Altar is at 'the head of the saint,' since the head of a corpse was always laid to the west. These phrases have already occurred in our quotations from the monkish chroniclers; for example, in the Saxon cathedral the matutinal altar was placed at the head of Dunstan, (p. 6), and Anselm, Odo, Wilfrid, and others, were deposited behind altars. On the other hand, in chantry chapels the tomb of the uncanonized founder is commonly at the west of the Altar, so that the priest stands at the foot of the tomb. The description of the shrine of St. Cuthbert at Durham will also serve to illustrate the two already mentioned. This too was placed behind the great reredos of the high Altar upon a raised platform inclosed, and forming what was called a 'feretory,' or chapel for the reception of a feretrum. This platform may still be seen extending partly into the great eastern transept, or 'Nine Altars,' as it is called. In the midst of it 'his sacred shrine was exalted with most curious workmanship of fine and costly green marble, all lined and gilt with gold, having four seats or places convenient underneath the shrine for the pilgrims or lame men setting on their knees to lean and rest on in the time of their devout offerings and fervent prayers to God, and holy S. Cuthbert for his miraculous relief and succour.' (Under the shrine of Edward the Confessor there are arches, three on each side, which probably served for a similar purpose.) 'At the west end of the shrine of S. Cuthbert was a little Altar adjoyned to it, for mass to be said only on the great and holy feast of S. Cuthbert's day in Lent... And at this Feast, and certain other festival dayes, in time of Divine Service, they were accustomed to draw up the cover of S. Cuthbert's shrine, being of wainscot, ... and a strong rope was fastened thereto, and did run up and down in a pulley under the vault for the drawing up of the cover: fine sounding silver Bells were fastened to the said rope, which at the drawing up of the cover made such a goodly sound, that it stirred all the peoples hearts within the church,' &c. This cover was painted and varnished within and without, and within the *feretory* on both north and south sides there were ambries of fine wainscot for relics (*Rites of Durham*).

Majesty had taken (particularly in his own church), for the images and bones of supposed saints to be taken away and defaced; which procured a royal letter, enjoining him to cause due search to be made in his cathedral churches, and if any shrine, covering of shrine, table, monument of miracles, or other pilgrimage, do there continue, to cause

Fig 47 Diaper, south side of choir.

it to be taken away, so as there remain no memory of it.'[t] And to these orders I suppose we must attribute the destruction of all those early monuments of the archbishops, of which we only know their ancient position; for unfortunately for the antiquarian, most of the early archbishops were either canonized or reputed saints. Even the tomb of Winchelsey was demolished about this time, because the people adored him as a reputed saint.[u]

The patriarchal chair which, until the last few years, stood upon the top of the steps at Y (fig. 5), and is there placed in Hollar's plan, was probably so fixed by English William upon the completion of Becket's chapel.

Behind the patriarchal chair the choir was parted from the chapel by a screen, which in Hollar's plan is extended between the pillars XI, and which Gostling describes as a 'fence of iron-work finished at the top with a rail or cornice of wood, painted with some of those ridiculous and trifling fancies with which the monks were every where fond of making the preaching orders of friars appear as contemptible as they could.'[x]

[t] Strype's *Memorials of Cranmer*, 92 ; Wilkins' *Concilia*, vol. iii. p. 858.

[u] This fact is recorded by Archbishop Parker, and therefore the tomb must have been demolished before the Rebellion (*De Antiq. Brit. Eccl.*, p. 317).

[x] Gostling, p. 261.

We now come to the disposition of the High Altar. In the old time there were three altars at the east part of the presbytery, namely, the high Altar in the middle, that of St. Elphege on the north, and of St. Dunstan on the south, with their respective shrines. The position of these altars may be pretty nearly determined, for the place of sepulture formally granted to Archbishop Bourchier,[y] is described as being between the two columns which are *nearest to the altar of St. Elphege,* (that is, columns VIII, IX on the north, for between these his monument stands). Also Archbishop Parker describes the monument of Stratford (33, fig. 5), as being near the high Altar on the south,[z] by *the steps of St. Dunstan's altar,* and that of Sudbury (31), as being on the *south side of the altar of St. Dunstan.*[a] The altars of Elphege and Dunstan were therefore placed at 19 and 32 respectively. There still remains between the monuments of Stratford and Sudbury some elegant diaper-work, which appears to have been part of the decoration of Dunstan's shrine.

The high Altar stood in Conrad's choir, nearly opposite to the window *s* (fig. 5), as Gervase tells us. It was also isolated, and behind it stood the patriarchal chair. In William's building, the piers VIII, IX were moved further eastward, and probably the Altar also. In the grant of a place of sepulture to Archbishop Bourchier (whose tomb stands at 18, fig. 5), it is especially required that no superfluous appendages shall be added to the monument, that may screen the light of the north windows from the altars.

In a sentence quoted below there occurs 'a screen of tabernacle-work richly overlaid with gold behind the communion table.' It appears from this that the high Altar did not remain isolated, but that a reredos had been placed behind it. The erection of this is not

---

y 'In spatio quod est in Boreali parte chori Ecclesiæ nostræ inter duas columnas proximas altari S. Elpheg' (Battely. App., p. iv)i.

z 'Ad summum altare in australi parte ad gradus altaris S. Dunstani in tumba alabastri honorifice sepultum est' (Parker, *de Antiq.,* p. 35).

a 'Ex parte australi altaris Dunstani sepultum est' (Do. p. 397). When Parker wrote, the position of these altars had not been forgotten.

recorded in the manuscripts of this church.[b] But many similar examples might be cited to shew that in the fourteenth and following centuries the high Altars of the ancient churches were no longer allowed to remain isolated, but that walls with rich tabernacle-work were erected in contact with their eastern faces, as, for example, at Peterborough, St. Alban's, Winchester, Durham, Westminster, &c. These walls had usually a door on each side of the high Altar, which led to the chapel or 'feretory' behind, as in the present instance. The reredos or 'Altar wall' in question extended between the pillars IX, and it is thus laid down in Hollar's plan, which was taken before the Rebellion. We have no record of the arrangements of the Altar after the Reformation until the time of Archbishop Laud. The removal of the shrines and altars of Dunstan and Elphege must have somewhat defaced this portion of the church. However, at the instigation of this Archbishop, considerable expense was bestowed upon ornaments and upon other matters in the neighbourhood

---

[b] In the list of Prior de Estria's works already quoted, there is an entry of payments, 'in various years for new vestments, and other ecclesiastical ornaments, and also a new 'tabula' for the high Altar, 147 *l.* 14 *s.*' (Galba E. IV. in Dart. App., p. iii). But this was probably a frontal. Again, Prior Chillenden ornamented the high Altar, and the two altars of St. Dunstan and St. Elphege with work of silver and gold, and wood curiously carved. ('Majus vero altare cum duobus altaribus sanctorum Dunstani et Elfegi opere argenteo aureo ac ligneo subtiliter inciso decenter ornavit' Ang. Sac. 143.) But this again may have only been frontal work, upon which great sums were often expended; for it is added that he also decorated three other altars with painting and wood-work, namely, the two on the north, of St. Stephen and St. Martin, and the one on the south, of St. John the Evangelist. But John Bokingham bishop of Lincoln, who died at Canterbury in 1397, in the days of this prior, gave twenty pounds towards building the high Altar (Dart, p. 90), which induces me to believe that the above entry refers to the erection of the reredos in question, since it shews that some considerable work was going on about the Altar. In the sixth volume of Leland's Itinerary are some notes concerning the monuments at Canterbury, which would have afforded some valuable information had they not unfortunately been contained in a portion of manuscript which has suffered so much from damp as to be nearly illegible, and the fragmentary sentences printed are in several cases so plainly wrong, that no dependance can be placed on them. However he distinctly mentions the 'waul of the High Altare.' This was the English name for the 'Reredos.' Heylyn, for example, gives the history of the removal of the 'altar wall' of St. Paul's in London by Bishop Ridley in 1550 (Heylyn's *Reformation*, p. 97).

of the Altar. The exact nature of the changes that were now introduced it is not easy to determine, for the only authorities on this
point are the Puritan writers, who are not much to be depended
upon. Prynne thus quotes a letter from the Dean to Archbishop
Laud: 'We have obeyed your Graces dircctions in pulling down
the exorbitant seates within our Quire whereby the church is very
much beautified. Lastly wee most humbly beseech your Grace to
take notice that many and most necessary have beene the occasions of extraordinary expences this yeare for ornaments of the Altar,' &c. (Dated July 8, 1634).[c] But whether the Altar rails were now
for the first time introduced,[d] as some of these writers say, may be
doubted. Culmer says that at 'the east end of the cathedral they
(the Dean and Chapter) have placed an Altar as they call it dressed
after the Romish fashion, for which Altar they have lately provided

c Prynne, *Canterburie's Doome*, p. 78.

d Prynne begins thus, (p.78) 'No sooner was this active prelate (Laud) promoted
to the Archbishopricke of Canterburie, but presently he began to pollute the Cathe-
drall of Canterbury with his popish innovations. First, hee caused an Altar to be there
erected by the Deane and Chapter, and much monies to bee expended by them upon
Basons, Candlesticks, Altar cloaths, and other furniture to adorne it, as appeares by
a letter written to him from the Deane and Chapter, (found in his study by Master
Prynne),' &c. (quoting as above). Heylyn merely says in his Life of Laud (p. 291), 'At
Canterbury Archbishop Laud found the table placed at the cast end of the choire by
the Dean and Chapter.' Neal in his *History of the Puritans*, boldly asserts that 'the
Cathedral of Canterbury was furnished (A.D. 1633), according to Bishop Andrews's
model, with two candlesticks,... ' (and other things enumerated in order, and concluding with) ' ... the footpace with three ascents covered with a Turkey carpet; three
chairs used at ordination, and the septum or rail, with two ascents' (*Hist. of the Puritans*, ch. 5. vol. ii.). But he is manifestly quoting merely the description of Laud's
chapel at Aberguilly, given by Prynne in *Canterburie's Doome* (p. 121). Wren, bishop
of Norwich, in his Answer to his Impeachment (1641) says, 'that rails and inclosures
before the Comunion table were not a thing newly or of late taken up; for in the
great churches of S. Paul, and of Westminster, of York, Norwich, and of divers other
Cathedral churches; also in S. Gregory's, S. Edmund's, S.Margaret's, and S. Michael's,
and other parish churches in Norwich, and in S. Margaret's at Westminster, S. Martin's
in Campis, S. Michael's in Crooked Lane, S. Saviour's, S. Giles' at Cripplegate, and
sundry more in London; these have been rails at the Communion table time out of
mind; at Hadley also, and Boxford, and Wilby, and many other churches of Norwich
Diocese' (*Parentalia*, p. 77).

a most idolatrous costly glory cloth or back cloth.'[e] These hangings were probably intended to cover the defacement of some imagery in the centre of the ancient reredos. However the Puritan troopers hewed the Altar rails in pieces in 1642, and 'threw the Altar over and over down the three Altar steps, and left it lying with the heels upwards.'[f] The church suffered exceedingly in the disorders that followed. 'The newly erected font was pulled down, the inscriptions, figures, and coats of arms, engraven upon brass, were torn off from the ancient monuments, and whatsoever there was of beauty or decency in the holy place, was despoiled.'[g]

These dilapidations are more particularly described in a manuscript drawn up in 1662, and preserved in the cathedral library.[h] 'The windows were generally battered and broken down; the whole roof, with that of the steeples, the chapter-house and cloister, extremely impaired and ruined both in timberwork and lead ; water-tables, pipes, and much other lead cut off; the choir stripped and robbed of her fair and goodly hangings; the organ and organ-loft, communion-table, and the best and chiefest of her furniture, with the rail before it, and the screen of tabernacle-work richly overlaid with gold behind it;[i] goodly monuments shamefully abused, defaced, and rified of brasses, iron grates, and bars, &c.'

After the Restoration a screen of the style then in use was erected in the same position as the old one, and the communion-table placed in front. The choir in this state is represented in Dart's view. But in 1729, the 'Altar-piece,' as it was called, had become old fashioned, and a bequest of £500 from one of the prebendaries was

---

e Culmer's Cathedral News.

f Culmer's Cathedral News.

g Battely's Preface to Somner.

h I quote this document from Britton, p. 39.

i The Puritans similarly destroyed the reredos of Peterborough in 1643, 'a stately skreen it was, well wrought, painted and gilt, which rose up as high almost as the roof of the church... This now had no imagery work upon it, or any thing else that might justly give offence, and yet because it bore the name of the high Altar, was pulled all down with ropes, lay'd low and level with the ground' Gunton, p.334.

expended upon a Corinthian screen, designed by Mr. Burrough, of Caius college, Cambridge, afterwards Master of that college; and at the same time wainscoting was carried from the Altar-piece to the two side doors of the choir. The choir in this state is represented in Wild's view.[k]

The original wooden stalls remained in the time of Somner, and he records that there were two rows on each side, an upper and a lower, and that above the stalls on the south side stood the archbishop's wooden seat or chair,[l] 'sometime richly guilt, and otherwise well set forth, but now nothing specious through age and late neglect. It is a close seat, made after the old fashion of such stalls, called thence *faldistoria;* only in this they differ, that they were moveable, this is fixt.'[m] But Somner wrote before the Rebellion, his book being published in 1640. However the stalls were not destroyed in the disorders, for they remained until 1704 when the present seats were substituted, and Archbishop Tenison gave a

k In these screens there were lateral doors leading to the chapel of the Trinity, and as this was the usual arrangement of a reredos they were probably imitated from the original one.

l The wooden seat of the archbishop in the choir 'sedem suam ligneam in choro,' is mentioned in the form of the inthronization (see the next note) in 1294. In the form of installing the prior, in the same MSS. however, the archbishop's place is termed the first stall of the quire on the south, 'in primo stallo chori ex parte australi.'

The prior's stall in the quire was on the north side, and in the chapterhouse the prior's place was close to the seat of the archbishop on the north (Form of electing and installing the Prior. Somner, App., p. 64) .

The form of the inthronization of Archbishop Winchelsey, A.D. 1294 (Somner, App. 57), contains some curious information respecting the arrangements of the choir, which I have extracted in the following abridgment:

The archbishop and prior, together with the convent, solemnly convey the pallium to the high Altar, and deposit it thereon. The convent remain in the choir, and the archbishop first remains prostrate in prayer before the high Altar, then proceeds to his wooden seat in the choir. After some other ceremonies, the archbishop wearing the pallium, the prior and six other ecclesiastics take their station, with their faces to the east, behind the high Altar, under the feretrum of St. Blaise, and in front of the marble chair. The king in the meantime stands near the said chair, with many of his nobles. Then the prior, leading the archbishop to the chair, inthrones him therein. And eight monks, under the shrine of St. Blaise, sing the Benedictus before the archbishop, seated in his throne. Lastly, he descends from his seat, and comes before the high Altar.

m Somner, p. 93.

throne of wainscot with a lofty canopy of the Corinthian order and carved by Gibbons." Queen Mary II provided the altar, archbishop's throne, stalls of the dean and vice-dean, and the pulpit, with new and rich furniture.º Now, however, all is again changed. The old Altar-table and screen are entirely taken away. A new reredos, imitated from the screen-work of the Lady Chapel in the crypt, has been erected in the place of the old screen of separation between the pillars XI (fig. 5), and the table set against it, near the old site of the patriarchal chair which is removed into the corona. Also the wainscoting which concealed the stone tracery of De Estria, has been removed from the sides of the choir, and Archbishop Tenison's throne replaced by a lofty canopy of tabernacle-work in stone; the pews still remain.

The organ has also had its changes of position. In the choir of Conrad it stood upon the vault of the south transept; afterwards it appears to have rested upon a large corbel of stone, over the arch of St. Michael's chapel, in the same transept. This corbel is represented in Britton's elevation, but has been since removed. In Dart's view, the organ is placed on the north side of the choir between the pillars III and IV. It was afterwards removed to the more common position over the west door of the choir.º Lastly, it has been ingeniously deposited out of sight in the triforium of the south aisle of the choir; a low pedestal with its keys stands in the choir itself, so as to place the organist close to the singers, as he ought to be, and the communication between the keys and the organ is effected by trackers passing under the pavement of the side aisles, and conducted up to the triforium, through a trunk let into the south wall.

The pavements and steps of the east end of the presbytery have undergone so many changes, that it is no easy task to discover the original arrangement, and yet the changes themselves are so curious as to deserve notice. The steps of Conrad's choir have been

n Gostling, p. 300.

o Battely, p. 94.

p Britton, pl. iv, shews the corbel above mentioned, and also the organ as it then stood over the screen.

exactly described by help of Gervase, but he says nothing about the steps of William's choir, and it is evident that the change of elevation of the pavement of Trinity chapel must have affected them.

In Hollar's plan, proceeding from the western door of the choir eastward, we first arrive at two steps extending between the two principal pillars (VI). The middle stone of the lower step has a semicircular projection, with a square hole in it now filled up. West of these steps, the pavement is of grey marble in small squares, but eastward is of large slabs of a peculiar stone, or veined marble, of a delicate brown colour.[q] When parts of this are taken up for repair or alteration, it is usual to find lead which has run between the joints of the slabs, and spread on each side below, and which is with great reason supposed to be the effect of the fire of 1174, which melted the lead of the roof, and caused it to run down between the paving stones in this manner.[r] This part of the pavement is consequently the undisturbed pavement of Conrad's choir, and probably the only part left.[s]

The two steps at VI. were removed three or four feet to the east of their original position in 1706, but the circular projection seems to have been intended for the reception of a crucifix, or a lectern, and therefore must have been part of the arrangement before the

q Gostling, p. 302.

r Gostling says that when the choir was pewed in 1706 some alterations were made in the pavement, and as much of that lead was picked up by some of the workmnl as made two large glue-pots (p. 246). And specimens of the same lead were obligingly placed on the table, by Mr. Austin, at the evening meeting of the Archæological Association at Canterbury in 1844.

s The exact boundary line between the presbyterium and choir of the monks may be doubtful. Gervase merely says that three steps divided them. I have laid down these steps at the pillars VIII, in fig. 3. Supposing the ancient pavement above described to be that of Conrad's choir, the steps at VI may be the site of the three steps in question, in which case they will be the boundary of the monk's choir. For although there are only two steps at present, the pavement of the choir has probably been raised; still Gervase may have omitted to mention these two steps. But I am inclined to think the presbytery extended to this point, by observing that Archbishop Parker, in describing the sites of monuments, calls the doors of entrance at this part the doors of the presbytery, and also says that Archbishop Chichely was buried on the north side of the presbytery.

Reformation. The level of the marble pavement in squares may, or may not, be the same as that of the original.

But the principal changes have been made in the pavement to the east of that just mentioned as being part of the original work of Conrad. In the first place, the removal of the two lateral altars of Dunstan and Elphege, with their platforms, must have made it necessary to relay and repair the pavement near them, and probably the upper steps were then carried across as they appear in Hollar's plan. This was drawn just before the Rebellion, and it contains three lines between VII and VIII, which either represent three steps, or more likely two steps and the altar-rails, which are known to have stood there. East of them is a narrow landing, and then four steps which lead to the platform of the communion-table.[t]

This arrangement was disturbed in 1732, when a new pavement of black and white marble was laid down, from the altar-rails to the Corinthian altar-piece then newly set up, as above described, and a single flight of six steps of white veined marble were introduced between VII and VIII, with an inscription to the donor, Mrs. Dorothy Nixon, and the date, 1732.[u]

The disposition of the screens and steps of the tower, which are so minutely described by Gervase, although they occupy part of the space of Lanfranc's building, yet must be held to belong to the works of Ernulf and Conrad, for the increased space eastward must have affected all the arrangement of the 'choir of the monks.' And there is good reason to suppose that the rood-screen with its lateral doors and the altar of the Holy Cross in the middle of its western face[x] may

---

t This is nearly consistent with Archbishop Laud's favourite arrangement, namely, the septum or rail, with two ascents, and then after a space a foot pace with three ascents to the table, which latter, however, had two steps only in his own chapel, and here appears to have had four steps.

u Gostling, p. 303.

x 'Altare S. Crucis in navi Ecelesie' occurs in the list of relics in Prior de Estria's register (Galba, E. 4. f. 122). This shews that it was not removed by the changes that took place after the fire of 1174. But there is no evidence to shew whether it was replaced after the rebuilding of the nave. Indeed Battely says that the registers mention an altar of the holy cross in the south part of the church (p. 27).

have remained, although probably in an altered form, even to the Reformation, as well as the Lady Chapel in the nave. In the account of the rebuilding of the nave by Prior Chillenden, to be examined in the next chapter, this Lady Chapel is expressly included. Erasmus, however, makes no mention of it, and it may have been removed when the Lady Chapel in the north transept was erected. One of Winchelsey's Statutes (A.D. 1298) expressly commands that the two small doors under the great loft, between the body of the church and the choir, which are near the altar under the great cross, shall remain closed, excepting it be necessary to open them for the service or for the egress and ingress of the ministers, or on occasion of the solemn processions.[y]

The same statute shews that the western entrance of the choir had remained up to this time open, for a strong injunction is given to the prior that he should immediately provide a handsome and strong wooden door for this entrance, with a good lock to it, so that it may be kept shut and locked at the proper times to prevent free access to the choir and upper parts of the church.[z] In fact the nave was completely shut off and the public excluded from those parts of the church that lay to the east of it by the doors and screens at B, E, and D (fig. 5). The account given by Erasmus shews that the mode by which strangers were conducted to these eastern parts was from the nave to the south transept, through the arch D (fig. 5),

[y] 'Ostia ferrea ante altare ad caput feretri sancti Thomæ, videlicet tam ex altaris opposito, quam etiam a latere boreali, una cum duobus ostiis minutis sub majori pulpito inter corpus ccelesiro et chorum per duo latera, juxta altare sub magna cruce ecelesiæ constitutis, elausa remaneant; nisi ratione divini officii vel ministerii egressus vel ingressus immineat necessarius, aut tempore peregrinationum solennium, de quibus superius tangitur, de permissione præsidentis expressa, hujusmodi ostia quandoque dimittantur aperta.'

[z] 'Item præcipimus et priori injungimus, ut statim, quam citius fieri poterit, opportulle,ostium pulchrum et forte ligneum cum forti et decente serura ad ingressum chori versus occidentem cum serura congrua construatur, ita quod claudi possit; et clausum ac servatum temporibus opportunis remaneat, ne per chorum liber ingressus pateat cuilibet transeunti, et ut superiori parti ecelesiæ, ubi magnum posset sæpius imminere periculum, major per hoc securitas præparetur' (Wilkins' Concilia, t. ii. p. 249).

and thence under the steps of the choir to the north transept: the Lady Chapel (as in fig. 3) probably cutting off the direct communication *B* (fig. 5) between the nave and the north transept. Gostling records that the strong iron grates and doors which parted the east end of the body and its side-aisles from the rest of the church, were removed about the middle of the eighteenth century.[a] The monks had their access to the church by means of the cloister door at *G*. But the martyrdom transept was separated from this entrance by a low wall (removed only in 1734,[b] and inserted in the plan fig. 5 on the authority of Hollar). A door at *H* gave access to this place from the cloister passage.

Durham cathedral resembles Canterbury in this respect, that the choir terminates at the eastern pillars of the central tower. From the description of its arrangements in the *Rites and Monuments* immediately before the Reformation, we learn that the western screen of the choir, between the *eastern* pillars of the tower, had the choir door in the middle as usual; an organ over it, and 'a lantern of wood, like unto a pulpit, standing and adjoyning to the wood organs over the quire door, where they had wont to sing the nine lessons in the old time on principal days, standing with their faces towards the high Altar.' But between the *western* pillars of the tower, 'over against the quire door, there was an altar called Jesus-altar, and on the back (eastern) side of that said altar was a fair high stone wall, and at either end of the wall a door; these were called the rood-doors for the procession. Over the wall was fixed the rood, and on the back side of it, before the quire door, a loft, and underneath the loft a long form, which did reach from one rood door to another, where men might sit to rest themselves, and say their prayers, and hear divine service.'[c]

Also two compartments of the south aisle of the nave of Durham, next to the cloister, were enclosed for the Neville Chapel.

a Gostling, p. 206.
b Ibid., p. 207.
c Abridged from the *Rites of Durham*, pp. 27, 54.

The most easterly was left for the passage for the cloister, and these were the next adjoining. The east end of the chapel, where the altar stood, was formed by a little stone wall somewhat higher than the altar, and wainscoted above the wall; the west end by a little stone wall, and the north side, towards the body of the church, environed with iron. The old Lady Chapel of Canterbury seems to have been very like this. The north aisle of Durham nave was separated from the transept by a *trellasdome,* or screen from pillar to pillar, with a door locked evermore, except for processions, as was the north rood door on the hither side of the pillar.

Comparing this with the ancient arrangement of Canterbury (fig. 3), we find that each had the choir wall with its door in the midst between the eastern tower piers, and also a second screen between the western tower piers, having a door at each end, an altar next to the nave in the middle, and the rood over it. The difference is, that in Canterbury, on account of the great crypt, there are steps between the two screens.

The visit of Erasmus to Canterbury cathedral is alluded to by all its historians, and is unfortunately too long and digressive to be given at length. I have already quoted it upon several occasions, and will conclude this section by endeavouring to abstract from it the order in which strangers were conducted over the cathedral at that time. He entered by the south porch, over which he observed the statues of the three knights who slew Thomas à Becket. In the nave he noted certain books fixed to the pillars, and amongst them the gospel of Nicodemus. Iron railing separated the nave from the space which was between that and the choir. Many steps ascended to this space, and under them a vaulted passage led to the north part (or transept) where he was shewn the small ancient wooden altar of the Virgin (p. 41 above). From this place he was conducted down to the crypt, and shewn the skull of St. Thomas and his ordinary garments. Then he returned and went to the choir, where on the north side he was shewn a multitude of relics, and examined the 'Tabula' and ornaments of the altar, and the riches beneath the altar, in the presence of which Midas and Crœsus would have seemed beggars. He was then led to the Sacrarium,[d] and the vestments, candlestick, &c. were shewn to him together with the staff of St. Thomas, his pallium and sudarium, which were only exhibited by special favour. After this he was taken to the upper part of the church, behind the high altar, where in a chapel (probably the corona) was the image of St. Thomas gilt and decorated with precious gems. In the next place the shrine was opened for his inspection, the prior pointing out with a white wand each jewel in succession, and mentioning its name, value, and the donor. Then he returned to the crypt, and was shewn the chapel of the Virgin and its riches; and lastly, was again brought to the sacrarium to see an old black chest filled with rags which had once belonged to Becket: he then took his leave. It is scarcely necessary to add, that the objects of his description were to expose the disgusting absurdities and evils of the system of relics, and to shew what vast riches were offered at their shrines.[e] His details therefore are confined to these matters, and other things neglected.

d This was probably the chapel of St. Andrew, which in Hollar's plan is marked as the vestiarium.

e The register of Prior Henry (Galba, E. IV. f. 122) contains a complete list of the relics preserved in the cathedral, and from the incidental mention of the places where they were deposited and the manner of their disposition, some information may be extracted concerning the arrangements at that period. Dart has printed the entire list (occupying nine pages), with some inaccuracies (Dart, App. No. XIII). It begins by enumerating the entire bodies of saints, then proceeds to detached heads and arms, and then to smaller bones, and such curiosities as pieces of Aaron's rod, and of the clay out of which Adam was made, also vestments, and fragments of vestments of divers saints, and portions of various objects of veneration from the Holy Land. I extract the list of the entire bodies and heads from the original.

'Reliquie
Corpus S^{ci} Thome martiris – In feretro suo (27, fig. 5)
Corpus S^{ci} Aelphegi – In feretro suo juxta magnum altare (19)
Corpus S^{ci} Dunstani - In feretro suo juxta magnum altare versus austrum (32)
Corpus S^{ci} Odonis – In feretro ad coronam versus austrum (23)
Corpus S^{ci} Wilfridi – In feratro ad coronam versus aquilonem (22)
Corpus S^{ci} Anselmi – In feretro ad altare Sancti Petri (29)
Corpus S^{ci} Aelfrici – Ad altare S^{ci} Johannis Evangelistæ (35)
Corpus S^{ci} Blasii – In feretro retro magnum altare (47)

The Crypt

Gervase says that the whole crypt of Ernulf was dedicated to the Virgin Mary. There were two chapels in the crypt especially

Corpus S^d Audoeni – In novo feretro in magna armariolo reliquarum
Corpus S^d Salvij – In primo feretro super trabem ultra magnum aHare
Corpus S^d Wlgani – In cista super trabem ultra altare S^{ci} Stephani (48)
Corpus S^d Swithuni -- In cista super trabem ultra altare set Martini (49)

In magno armariolo reliquarum juxta magnum altare continentur
Caput S^d Blasii – in capite argenteo et deaurato
Caput S^d Fursei – in capite argenteo et deaurato et amaHato
Caput S^d Austroberte – in capite argenteo amaliato et deaurato.'
&c. &c. &c.

Then follow twelve detached arms of divers saints 'in brachiis argenteis et deauratis' and so on. The list concludes with the enumeration of certain miscellaneous relics contained 'in primo, secundo et tertio feretro, super trabem ultra magnum altare' – 'in armariolo retro magnum altare' – 'in majori cornu eburneo* pendente sub trabe ultra magnum altare' – 'in lectrino ligneo ad altare sanctæ crucis in navi Ecclesie, in parte cooperta argento deaurato, cum gemmis, cum cruce in medio,' &c. &c.

Most of the saints in the above list have occurred in the course of the history, and I have accordingly added references to the plan fig. 5. St. Audoen (pp.4, 46) was deposited in the time of Gervase in the crypt, under the altar of St. Gregory, whence he appears by this list to have been removed to the great relic cupboard at the high Altar. Prior Goldston (c. 1500) made a new feretrum for him. 'Feretrum etiam sanctissimi Audoeni in quo ejusdem reliquiæ reverenter sunt reconditæ de opere ligneo decenter inciso ac deaurato fieri fecit' (Obit. in Ang. Sac., tom. i, p. 147). He also gave a brazen eagle to the church. 'Analogium quoque sive Aquilam æneam propriis expensis procurari fecit,' and three pieces of hangings of 'Arysse,' embroidered with the history of the Virgin, which were suspended on the south side of the choir at certain times of the year. 'Tres etiam pannos pulcherrimos opere de Arysse subtiliter intextos, ortum Virginis cum vita et obitu ejusdem clare et splendide configurantes, in parte chori australi certis temporibus anni fecit appendi.' We need not be surprised to find in the above list the body of St. Blaise in one place and his head in another. When the coffin of Dunstan was opened (p. 59 above) a piece of his skull was taken out as a memorial and put into the hands of the prior (the same Goldston), who enclosed it in a receptacle of silver (massa argentea) made in the shape of a head, which was preserved amongst the relics of the church. This was commonly denominated St. Dunstan's head, 'massam argenteam in formam capitis dictus Prior decenter ac satis artificiose fabricari fecit; in quo eandem portiunculam capitis satis honorifice ac reverenter fecit collocari; ipsumque inter Reliquias Ecclesie, ut decuit voluit conservari. Quod quidem ab omnibus caput S. Dunstani vulgariter nuncupatur' (Ang. Sac., p. 147). The heads of St. Furseus and St. Austroberta were anciently enclosed in the altars of the Saxon cathedral (pp. 12, 13 above), and so also was the *head* of St. Swithun, but this list claims the *body* of that saint, which was also said to be preserved at Winchester. No record tells

*CORNU. Vas Ecclesiasticum… *Cornua 2 eburnea reliquis conferta'* &c. (Ducange).

dedicated to her, namely, the central one under the high Altar, and the south transept which was fitted up for a chantry founded by the Black Prince in A.D. 1363, and endowed for the maintenance of two priests. The original Norman vault of this transept has been replaced by a *lierne*[e] vault and the walls clothed with masonry, so as to transform the whole into the style of the period at which the chantry was founded. This chapel is now appropriated to the use of

us how St. Salvius and St. Wlganus were acquired; the first was a bishop of Albi, and died A.D. 584. In a list of 'Saints, Martyrs, Confessors, and Virgins, whose bodies rest in the metropolitan church' (Claud. B. ix. f. 265. Dart, xxvi), I find 'Sanctus Vulganius Sacerdos et Confessor,' which is all that appears to be known of him. The great relic cupboard was on the north side, as Erasmus tells us. It was probably in the feretory behind the reredos. In St. Paul's, London, the feretrum of St. Erkenwald was placed in the middle of the east side of the altar wall, exactly behind the high Altar (see Dugdale's Plan, and pp. 24, 114), in a position exactly corresponding to that of St. Blaise at Canterbury. However a priest officiating at the altar of St.Erkenwald would have faced the west. In the chartulary of St. Augustine's preserved in the library of Trinity Hall, Cambridge, there is a very curious drawing representing the arrangement of the high Altar of that church, which from its neighbourhood to the cathedral was probably somewhat similar to it in many respects. This drawing has been engraved by Somner and Dugdale. There is some difficulty in properly translating its meaning on account of the part plan, part rude perspective, manner in which it is drawn. As I understand it, it represents the reredos of the high Altar with the feretory behind it. The three semicircles are the pier-arches of the apse, in each of which an altar is placed against the end of a shrine. The lateral shrines, however, are not placed in the east and west direction, but lie either north and south, or, as I rather believe, are intended to radiate with the apse, so as to lie north-east and south-east respectively; ten other smaller shrines or monuments without altars are distributed between the three principal ones. The reredos (apparently in the Decorated style or later) has a battlemented crest, a niche or door on each side, close to the altar (perhaps of an ambrey)' and at each extremity a door inscribed as leading to the bodies of the saints behind. The shrine of St. Ethelbert rests on the crest of the reredos in the centre, thus being placed 'retro magnum altare,' like St. Blaise and St. Erkenwald; and some other relics appear at the sides, amongst which are the books sent by Pope Gregory to Augustine, and two arms, probably 'brachia argentea,' containing bones. Two short columns also stand on the battlemented crest, and help to support the 'beam' above. In the midst of this is the 'majestatem Domini,' with an angel on each side, and two reliquary chests. This evidently resembles in many particulars the disposition of the high Altar of the cathedral (See Hickes' *Thesaurus*, ii, 172).

e Namely, a vault in which short transverse ribs or 'liernes' are mixed with the ribs that branch from the vaulting capitals. (See *Trans. of Institute of Brit. Arch.*, vol. i. p. 2).

f See Somner, p. 97, and App. 31; Gostling, p. 216.

a congregation of French refugees, who firſt came to Canterbury in the time of Edward VI. The crypt was granted to them by Queen Elizabeth.ʄ The chapel of the Virgin in the middle of the crypt is enclosed with screen-work, the date of which is loſt. The vault of the crypt of the corona retains the initials J and M, so that on the whole it seems that the crypt was to the laſt dedicated to the Virgin Mary.

The Window of Anselm's Chapel

In Anselm's chapel, the original window of the south wall has been taken out and replaced by a very large and elaborate Decorated window of five lights, which is remarkable for its well-preserved hiſtory; this is contained in the following document, printed by Battely, from the Archives:ᵍ 'Memorandum, that in the year 1336, there was made a new window in Chriſt Church, Canterbury, that is to say, in the chapel of the Apoſtles, Sts. Peter and Paul, upon which there were expended the sums following:

	£.	s.	d.
Imprimis, for the workmanship only, or labour of the masons	21	17	9
Item, for the taking down of the wall where the window was placed	0	16	9
—— for lime and gravel	1	0	0
—— for 20 cwt. of iron bought for the said window	4	4	0
—— for the labour of the smith	3	5	4
—— for Caen ſtone bought for the same	5	0	0
—— for glass, and the labour of the glaziers	6	13	4
	42	17	2

The sum of £8. 13s. 4d. was given by certain friends for the said window, and the remainder of the money was furnished by the prior.'

This prior was Henry de Eſtria, and the peculiar management of the heads of the lights, with their pendent bosses, may be compared with the similar bosses of his choir door (figs. 44, 45, above).

The interior of this tracery is in very good preservation, with the exception of the pendent bosses, and the stones whence they were suspended, which have totally disappeared. The outside of the window is, however, in a very bad condition for the purpose of the antiquarian; for, apparently on account of the decayed state of its surface, the tracery has undergone the process of splitting, namely, the whole of the outer part has been pared down to the glass, and fresh worked in Portland stone; Portland stone mullions, or monials as they are more properly called, have also been supplied. And as this repair was executed at a period when this class of architecture was ill understood, the moldings were very badly wrought, which, in conjunction with the unfortunate colour and surface of the Portland stone, has given the window a most ungenuine air. However, the interior is as good as ever it was, and it is on account of its date, as well as for its beauty, a most valuable example.

There are some peculiarities in the manner of distributing the moldings of this window which are shewn in the figures. The heads of the lights are worked with different moldings from those of the

g 'Memorand. Quod anno 1336 facta fuit una fenestra nova in Ecclesia Christi Cant. viz. in capella S. S. Petri et Pauli Apostolorum, pro quo expensæ fuerant ministratæ.

	l.	*s.*	*d.*
Impr. pro solo Artificio seu labore Cementariorum	xxi	xvii	ix
Item pro muri fractione ubi est fenestra		xvi	ix
—— pro sabulo et calce		xx	
—— pro M. M. ferri empti ad dictam fenestram		lxxxiv	
—— pro artificio Fabrorum		lxv	iv
—— pro lapidibus Cani emptis ad eandem		c	
—— pro vitro et labore vitraii	vi	xiii	iv
	xlii	xvii	ii

Summa viii*l.* xiii*s.* iv*d.* data fuit a quibusdam amicis ad dictam Fenestram. Reliqua pecunia ministrata fuit a Priore.' Ex: Archivis Eccles. Cant. (Battely, App. 1).

Fig. 48 Window in Anselm's chapel.

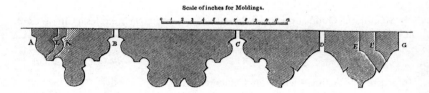

Fig. 49 Section of moldings of ditto.

tracery above, and the increased size and importance of the two central monials are given, not by an additional layer or order of moldings, as usual, but by separating the other moldings.

Chapter 7

THE HISTORY OF THE NAVE, TOWER, AND WESTERN
TRANSEPTS, FROM THE END OF THE TWELFTH CENTURY

THE CONCLUSION OF GERVASE'S HISTORY leaves the original nave
and transepts of Lanfranc untouched, and thus they appear to have
remained until the end of the fourteenth century, when they were
taken down and replaced as we now see them. The history of this
change, and of the subsequent works, must be gathered from various detached documents, for we have no longer a continuous narrative to depend upon like that of Gervase; I shall therefore proceed to extract from these documents as much as is necessary for
the history of the building, adding also a concise description of the
parts of the building in question.

1. The Nave

In December of the year 1378, Archbishop Sudbury issued a mandate addressed to all ecclesiastical persons in his diocese enjoining
them to solicit subscriptions for rebuilding the nave of the church,
and granting forty days' indulgence to all contributors. The preamble states that the nave, on account of its notorious and evident
state of ruin, must necessarily be totally rebuilt, that the work was
already begun, and that funds were wanting to complete it.[h] In the
year 1397, Archbishop Arundell appropriated to the convent the
parsonages of Godmersham and Westwell, in Kent, at their peti-

---

[h] 'Sane cum navis dictæ ecclesiæ nostræ Cant. metropoliticæ, propter ipsius no-
toriam et evidentem ruinam, de novo oporteat totaliter construi, et etiam reparari;
sitque jam notorie ipsa navis in construendo, ad cujus operis consummationem ipsius
ecclesiæ sine Christi fidelium subventione et auxilio propriæ non suppetunt facul-
tates,' &c. (Ex Reg. Sudbury, fol. 52a, Wilkins' *Concilia*, t. iii. p. 136).

tion. The preface to the instrument of appropriation (dated in the above year) expressly states the reasons for this grant to be that 'Simon of Sudbury, formerly archbishop of Canterbury, and our predecessor, had caused the nave of our church to be taken down to the foundation and demolished at his own expense, for the purpose of re-erecting the same, as he intended, and fervently desired, to do, but was prevented by his violent death (on June 15, 1381); and that the prior and convent had laudably expended upwards of five thousand marks out of their common property, upon the construction of the said nave and other necessary works about the church. Also, that six thousand marks would be too little to finish the work as begun, and others that must be done about the prostrate cloister and the chapter-house, which is thought to be in a dangerous state;' and he also states as a reason for thus augmenting their funds, his wish that so laudable and necessary a work should be carried on, lest its final completion might be retarded 'by the loss of the present prior,' or by other adverse circumstances.[i]

A.D. 1381–96 In the Obituary it is recorded that Archbishop Courtney[k] gave more than a thousand marks to the fabric of the nave of A.D. 1396–1413 the church, the cloister, &c.; and that Archbishop Arundell[l] gave five sweet sounding bells, commonly called 'Arundell ryng,' as well as a thousand marks to the fabric of the nave.[m]

i '... cum bonæ memoriæ Dominus Simon de Sudburia quondam Arch. Cant. prædecessor noster navem præfatæ nostræ ecclesiæ prosterni fecerat funditus, et suis sumptibus demoliri, causa ipsam erigendi de novo prout proposuit et fervente optavit, si non per Dei emulos fuisset inaudita per prius populi furoris audacia decollatus. Vosque Prior et Capitulum circa constructionem navis prædictæ, et alia necessaria opera ejusdem ecclesiæ nostræ de communibus bonis vestris ultra quinque millia marcarum laudabiliter expenderitis... quodque incepta opera et alia inibi de necessitate fienda prostrati claustri vestri et capitularis Domus vestræ pensata imminente ruina cumsex millibus marcarum perfici nequeant et reparari decenter, attenta hospitalitate Dominorum et aliorum diversorum Regnorum apud vos indies confluentium quam declinare non poteritis cum honore,' &c. Somner, p. 89, and App. p.24.

k W. Courtney, Archbishop. 'Ad fabricam navis Ecclesiæ, claustri et murorum clausuram circa gardinum Celerarii mille marcas et ultra suâ gratiâ contulit.' Obit., *Ang. Sac.*, p. 61.

A.D.
1390–1411
Of Prior Chillenden,[n] the same document states that 'he, by the help and assistance of the Rev. Father Thomas Arundell, did entirely rebuild the nave of the church, together with the chapel of the Blessed Virgin Mary, therein situated, and handsomely constructed.' Also the cloister, chapter-house, and other buildings enumerated.

The epitaph of this prior, preserved by Somner, confirms this statement, by saying, 'Here lieth Thomas Chyllindenne, formerly Prior of this Church... who reconstructed the nave of the Church and divers other buildings... and who, after holding the priorate twenty years, twenty-five weeks, and five days, completed his last day on the assumption of the Blessed Virgin, (Aug. 25) A.D. 1411.'[o]

The history of the nave resembles that of the choir of Ernulf, in this respect, that the archbishops assisted the work with funds and influence, but that it was really carried on by the convent under the immediate direction of the prior. It is not even certain that the prior was the actual architect in either of these instances; for in those times; as in our own, men in high official situations were to be found, who took the greatest pleasure in promoting the erection of buildings, and assisted in the carrying on of the works in various

l T. Arundell, Archbishop. 'Contulit huic Ecclesiæ... quinque campanas in sonitu dulcissimas Arundell ryng vulgariter nuncupatas... Contulit etiam ad fabricam navis Ecclesiæ mille marcas.' Obit., *Ang. Sac.,* p. 62.

m Leland says 'King Henry the 4th and he (namely Arundel) helpid to build up a good part of the Body of the Chirch.' *Itin.,* vol. vi. fol. 3.

n T. Chillenden, Prior. 'Qui ope et auxilio Rev[i]. Patri T. Arundell .... navem istius Ecclesiæ cum Capellâ B. Mariæ Virginis in eâdem sitâ opereque decenti fabricatâ totaliter renovavit. Claustrum quoque, Domum Capitularem, magnum Dormitorium cum novâ viâ versus Ecclesiam, et subtus domum rasturæ, de novo fieri fecit...' Various other works and buildings are also enumerated. Obit., *Ang. Sac.,* p. 143.

o The entire epitaph is as follows: 'Hic jacet Dominus Thomas Chyllindenne quondam Prior hujus Ecclesiæ, Decretorum Doctor egregius, qui navem istius Ecclesiæ cæteraque diversa redificia, quamplurima quoque opera laudabilia de novo fieri fecit. Pretiosa insuper – ecclesiastica, multaque privilegia insignia huic Ecclesie acquisivit, qui postquam Prioratum hujus Ecclesiæ annis viginti. 25. septimanis, et quinque diebus nobiliter rexisset, tandem in die assumptionis beatæ Mariæ Virginis diem suum clausit extremum. Anno Domini 1411. Cujus animæ propitietur Deus. Amen.' Somner, App. p. 62.

ways, by advising, criticising, furnishing funds, and cheering on the proceedings by continual countenance and sanction. And to such men, the credit of the enterprize may very justly be attributed, but not the credit of the design artistically speaking. This was often due to some obscure monk, or workman, whose name has been lost. For example, Matthew Paris records that a new roof was formed of oak for the aisles of the church of St. Alban's, as well as for the tower, and substantially covered with lead, all which was done at the instigation, and by the labour of, Michael of Thydenhanger, monk and camerarius. Nevertheless, he adds: these works must be ascribed to the abbot, out of respect to his office, for he who sanctions the performance of a thing by his authority, is really the person who does the thing.*p* This doctrine, however true it may be in the sense in which the author intends it to be taken, is fatal to the history of art; for it has been largely acted upon by the monkish chroniclers, who attribute architectural works, without reserve, to the bishop or prior whose biography they are writing, when in reality these labours were carried on by the monks, and directed by artists whose names, with few exceptions, are lost.

The nave, transepts, and pillars of the central tower of Canterbury, all evidently belong to the same period, and constitute one work, for they are all in the same style and of the same design (except of course the buttressing arches and additions to the tower piers, of which more below). The work of the nave, therefore, above mentioned, must be held to include these transepts. The documents

p M. Paris, Vit. S. Alb. Abb. p. 1054.

q In the life of Simon Sudbury, which Wharton has extracted from the Speculum Parvulorum, and which he tells us is the work of William Chartham, a monk of Canterbury in 1448 (*Ang. Sac.*, tom. i. pp. xx. and 49), it is related that Sudbury built 'two aisles in the posterior' (i. e. western) 'part of the church,' 'duas alas enim in parte posteriori ejusdem Ecclesiæ necnon Portam Occidentalem Civitatis à fundamentis et muros ejusdem tunc quasi præcipites erexit, et fieri fecit sumptibus propriis et expensis.' These must be the aisles of the nave which were probably begun before the death of Sudbury, and perhaps carried on afterwards from his funds. However the Obituary, which minutely records the works of other archbishops, is silent with respect to Sudbury's. Battely and others take these aisles to be the transepts.

Fig. 50 Compartment of nave.

just quoted, which in fact contain all that is known upon the subject, have told us that Archbishop Sudbury pulled down the nave
about 1378 on account of its ruinous condition, intending to rebuild
it, but was prevented by his death in 1381,[q] and that the succeeding
archbishops, Courtney and Arundell, contributed largely to the

funds. Prior Chillenden, who held that office from 1390 to 1411, seems to have been the most active person in conducting these and other buildings, and is thus alluded to in the Arundell grant.

This grant is dated in the second year of Arundell's archbishopric, and the seventh of Chillenden's priorate, and the works seem then to have been in a great state of forwardness, but our information fails to give us the real architect, or the exact year at which they were commenced, and from which the design must be dated. Nine years intervened between the death of Sudbury and the beginning of Chillenden's priorate; but he may have conducted the works in the meantime in some other monastic office.

When the rebuilding of the nave and transepts was undertaken, the portion they were designed to replace was the original nave and transepts of Lanfranc; this was considerably lower than the eastern church. In the section fig. 6. *BC* is the level of Lanfranc's ceiling, and the dotted semicircle *D* shews the position of his tower-arch. Now in the nave, the whole of Lanfranc's piers, and all that rested on them, appear to have been utterly demolished, nothing remaining but the plinth of the side aisle walls. In the transepts more parts of the Norman wall were allowed to remain, especially on the eastern side, and at the angles; and of the tower piers the western are probably mere casings of the original, and the eastern certainly appendages to the original as already shewn at *F,* fig. 13. p. 77. But of course it must be understood that I have no evidence to shew how much of Lanfranc's pier was allowed to remain in the heart of the work. The interior faces of the tower walls appear to have been brought forward by a lining so as to increase their thickness and the strength of the piers, with a view to the erection of a lofty tower, which however was not carried above the roof until another century had nearly elapsed. One compartment of the nave is shewn in fig. 50. Fig. 51 is a plan of the pier, and fig. 52^r the section of the jamb. The style is light Perpendicular, and the arrangement of the parts has considerable resemblance to that of the nave of Winchester, although the latter is of a much bolder character. Winchester nave was going on at the

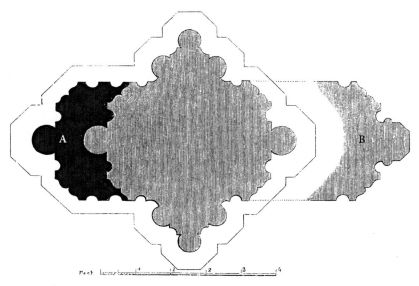

Fig. 51 Plan of a pier of the nave. **A** the additional portions next to the tower; **B** the arch mold.

same time with Canterbury nave, and a similar uncertainty exists about the exact commencement. In both a Norman nave was to be transformed, but at Winchester the original piers were either clothed with new ashlaring, or the old ashlaring was wrought into new forms and moldings where possible; while in Canterbury the piers were altogether rebuilt. Hence the piers of Winchester are much more massive. The side-aisles of Canterbury are higher in proportion, the

Fig. 52 Section of the window jamb of the side-aisles.

r In fig. 51 the plan line of the plinth was laid down from the half pier of the tower, in which the plinths are double; this line is therefore more distant from the body of the pier than it ought to be to represent the plinths of the other piers of the nave, which are all single.

tracery of the side-windows different, but those of the clerestory are almost identical in pattern, although they differ in the management of the moldings. Both have 'lierne' vaults,[s] and in both the triforium is obtained by prolonging the clerestory windows downward and making panels of the lower lights, which panels have a plain opening cut through them, by which the triforium space communicates with the passage over the roof of the side-aisles.

2. *The Lady Chapel, South-West Tower, and Chapel of St Michael*

The Obituary records of Prior Goldston, that 'he built on the north side of the church a chapel in honour of the Blessed Virgin Mary, in which he was buried.[t] He completely finished this chapel, with a stone vault of most artificial construction, a leaden roof, glass windows, and all other things belonging to it. He also constructed the walls of the court-yard, 'atrium,' of the said chapel, with a lead roof but no vault.' – 'Moreover, he finished with beautiful workmanship the tower or campanile which was on the south part of the nave; from the height of the side-aisle of the church upward.'

A.D. 1449–68

This chapel (marked LADY CHAPEL in fig. 5) occupies the site of the apsidal chapel of St. Benedict, but extends considerably farther to the east; it is now called the Dean's chapel. The vault is a fan vault, and differs in that respect from the other vaults of the western portion, which are of the class which I have denominated lierne vaults. This was the first large fan vault that had been executed in this cathedral,

---

s See note *e*, p. 129.

t T. Goldston, Prior. 'Ædificavit in Boreali parte hujus Ecclesiæ Capellam in honorem B. V. Mariæ, in qua et sepultus est. Quam videlicet Capellam cum testudine lapideâ valde artificiosâ, coopertura et plumbo, fenestris vitreatis et aliis omnibus ad eum pertinentibus complevit. 'Atrii quoque ejusdem Capellæ parietes cum coopertura de plumbo absque testudine construxit.'

'Turrem quoque sive campanile in australi parte navis Ecclesie ab altitudine porticus Ecclesie supra pulchro artificio consummari fecit.' (MS. Arundel. 68. Plut. clxiii. F). Wharton has obscured this passage by printing *ad altitudinem* instead of the *ab altitudine* of the original (*Ang. Sac.*, i. 145).

and is therefore distinguished in the above narrative.[u] A similar vault is introduced in the south-west campanile above mentioned.

What is said of the 'atrium' of the chapel is not very intelligible, but I presume it refers to the passage on the north which lies between the chapter-house and the said chapel. An elegant screen separates the chapel from the 'Martyrdom' or north transept, and is well represented in the engravings referred to in the note.[x]

In the south transept the old chapel of St. Michael has been replaced by one which corresponds in position and nearly in dimensions with that of our Lady just described. The builder of it is not recorded. The style of it is Perpendicular, and with no greater differences from the former than might be expected from the works of two artists. But the vault is quite different, and is a complex lierne vault of an unusual pattern,[y] but resembling that of the north transept of Gloucester cathedral, which dates from 1367 to 1372. Leland styles the chapel in question 'St. Annes Chapelle'.

In the middle of the chapel is a monument which was erected by Margaret Holland to the memory of her two husbands, John Beaufort earl of Somerset, who died in 1410, and Thomas duke of Clarence, who died in 1420. As she died in 1437 the monument was erected between 1420 and 1437, and we may presume that the present chapel was then in existence. Leland indeed says, 'This chapel be likelihod was made new for the Honor of Erle John of Somerset. In the south Wyndowes of the same goodly chapel be written yn the Glasse Wyndowes these 3 Name, John Counte of Somerset, The Lorde Percy, The Lord Mortaine, and everyone with the Kings Armes.'[z]

---

u The small chantry chapel (*n*, fig. 5) on the north of Trinity chapel, is usually attributed to Henry IV., whose tomb it is close to. He in his will founds a 'chauntre perpetuall of twey preestis for to sing and pray for my soul,' and died 1412. This chapel is 14ft by 8ft, and it has a rich little fan vault. But the Lady chapel is much larger, namely, 39ft by 21ft.

x For engravings of this chapel, see Wild, pl. 4; Britton, pl. 8, 26. For the western tower, see Wild, pl. 1; Britton, pl. 3, 6.

y The plan of one compartment of this vault is drawn in fig. 5.

z Lel. Itin., vol. vi. fol. 3. He says of Cardinal Langton that he 'made, as I harde, the stately Horologe in the South crossid Isle of the Chirche.'

There is a plain vaulted apartment above this chapel which is reached by the long staircase already mentioned (p. 108). Three inscriptions appear at the keystones of the vault; 'the eastern one has remaining Tho——— prior, the middle one seems to have been Johns Wodnesbergh, the western one Willms Molasch discipulus.'[a] Now Prior Thomas Chillenden was succeeded by John Wodnesburgh in 1411, and he by William Molasch in 1427, so that as the inscriptions indicate that neither of the latter were priors when they were written, we may venture with Gostling to fill up the first blank with Chillenden, and thus assign the entire chapel to his time. In all probability it formed part of the general scheme for the transformation of the western part of the church, for it was obviously impossible that the Norman apses should not have been included in the proposed changes, although, as in the case of the northern one, the rebuilding of them might have been postponed for a few years to make way for more essential portions of the building, or (as is sometimes the case even now) they might have been reserved as likely works to tempt the generosity of individual benefactors.

3. The Central Tower, or Angel Steeple

In the year 1495 Prior Sellyng was succeeded by a second Thomas Goldston, who like his namesake was a great builder, and the obituary records many works of his. But that which he added to the church will be best stated in the exact words of the original.[b]

A.D. 1495 -1517

a I quote them from Gostling, p. 251, as they were then rather more legible; however they still remain as he records them.

b 'Turrim satis excelsam Angyll Stepyll vulgariter nuncupatam, testudine pulcherrimâ concameratam ac opere decenti artificiose undique sculptam et deauratam, cum fenestris vitreatis satis amplis et ferramentis, ope et auxilio... Rev[i]. Patris J. Morton Cardinalis necnon et Dom[i]. W. Sellyng Prioris, in medio Ecclesiæ vid[t]. inter chorum et navem Ecclesiæ, egregie erexit et magnifice consummavit. Duos etiam arcus sive fornices opere lapideo subtiliter incisos cum quatuor aliis minoribus ad sustentationem dictæ Turris columnis eandem Turrim supportantibus satis industrie et prudenter annexit...' Ang. Sac., t. i, p. 147.

'He by the influence and help of those honourable men, Cardinal John Morton and Prior William Sellyng, erected and magnificently completed that lofty tower commonly called Angyll Stepyll in the midst of the church, between the choir and the nave – vaulted with a most beautiful vault, and with excellent and artistic workmanship in every part sculptured and gilt, with ample windows glazed and ironed. He also with great care and industry annexed to the columns which support the same tower, two arches or vaults of stone work, curiously carved, and four smaller ones, to assist in sustaining the said tower.'

And of Cardinal Morton the same obituary states, that 'with his _{A.D.} help and at his expense great part of the tower in the middle of the church was erected.'[c]

A.D.
1486–1501

As Goldston is said to have been assisted by Prior Sellyng in the work, he must have undertaken it before he obtained the priorate. By erecting the tower is plainly meant only that part which rises above the roof, for the fact that he added the buttressing arches to the piers, shews that the piers were there before. And the masonry of these arches indicates very plainly that they are insertions, and that the piers had been transformed into the Perpendicular style long before. It is probable that the piers shewed some signs of weakness, which induced this somewhat disfiguring addition, and indeed the north-west pier which is not so completely fortified as the rest is now considerably bowed in the middle towards the east. For the two great arches above mentioned are inserted under the western and southern tower-arches respectively (E and F, fig. 5). The eastern arch having stronger piers did not require this precaution, and the northern, which opened upon the 'Martyrium,' seems to have been left free out of reverence to the altar of the martyrdom, and accordingly to have suffered the dislocation just mentioned. In the section I have inserted the arch (A, fig. 6), which really belongs to the opposite arch (F, fig. 5), having no other way of shewing the extent

c 'Sui denique ope sumptibusque magna pars Turris in Ecclesiæ medio constructa est.' *Ang. Sac.*, t. i, p. 63.

and manner of this buttressing. The four smaller arches marked *A, B, C, D,* in the plan, are employed to connect the two great western tower-piers with the wall of the transept and with the nearest nave-pier respectively. The nature of their insertion is shewn in the section (*a b c d,* fig. 5), and it appears that not only is this flying arch introduced at mid-height of the pier, but that the piers themselves are strengthened by an addition, which contracts the span of the arch to *a b,* and that the pier-arch over head, is also contracted in dimensions and in altitude by the substitution of a smaller and lower arch for the original, the extent and manner of which change is shewn by the dotted outlines at *c d.* The plan of the nave-pier, fig. 51. p. 139, shews at A the comparative magnitude of this addition as well as the moldings by which it is ornamented; the vertical joint of separation between the two works is too plain to be mistaken in all the piers in which this addition oocurs.

The buttressing arches consist of a strong and singular reticulated masonry, admirably adapted for the purpose, and have the rebus of Thomas Goldston, namely, a shield with three gold stones. The central western buttressing arch (*E,* fig. 5) occupies the place of the ancient rood-loft, and probably the great rood was placed over it until the Reformation, so that the intrusive effect which it now produces would not have been felt when it was erected, because the great arch had never been left open.[d]

d These buttressing arches are represented in most of the modern works relating to this cathedral (as in Britton, pl. 16; Wild, pl. 1; Woolnoth, pl. 12; and Winkles, pl. 9). There is an excellent elevation in Britton, pl. 14, which is well calculated to shew these arches and their relative position and magnitude to the choir-screen, and tower-arch above.

Chapter 8

Properly speaking the monuments form no part of my plan, for to describe them would require a great number of drawings, and extend this work greatly beyond its proposed limits. But few cathedrals possess so interesting a series, and as Gervase has so minutely described the burial-places of all the archbishops up to his period, I shall give a list of the archbishops, shewing their known resting-places in the church, and mention the monuments that remain.

Unfortunately, out of fifty archbishops and distinguished personages before the Reformation, the locality of whose tombs or shrines have been recorded, only about eighteen monuments are left, many of which are in a greater or less state of dilapidation. With one exception, however, they are all securely appropriated to their respective owners, and thus dated, which greatly increases their value and use for the history of art. Their positions were so minutely described by Archbishop Parker at a period when all the inscriptions remained, that there can be no mistake in this respect.

The exception just mentioned is a tomb which now stands on the south side of the Trinity chapel, (24, fig. 5); its sides are decorated with an arcade of trefoil arches, resting on shafts which have round abacuses and bases, and the style seems a little later than the completion of the Trinity chapel. No record of a monument on this spot is preserved, and if, as is probable, it has been removed from its original site, all clue to its history is gone. It may have been constructed after the completion of the church, to receive the bones of some of the archbishops who had been removed. It is usually attributed to Archbishop Theodbold (3, fig. 5), but without reason, and is too late in style.

The panelling below the effigy of Hubert Walter (40) is manifestly a much later construction, and the stone coffin (42) attributed to Stephen Langton, which is now built into the wall of the chapel of St. Michael, seems to have been originally outside the wall, in the church-yard; and thus the new wall, when the chapel was rebuilt and enlarged in the fourteenth century, was made to stride over the coffin by means of an arch. The earliest complete monument in the cathedral is that of John Peckham, who died A.D. 1292, (4).[e] For Walter Reynolds (40) there only remains some insignificant panelling below the effigy, which is probably, like that of Hubert Walter, which is close to it, part of the fitting up of a chantry chapel.

The memorial of Archbishop Mepham, who died in 1333, is a beautiful and singular work, consisting of an altar-tomb, placed between a double arcade, which forms the screen of Anselm's chapel, at 28 in the plan.

Archbishop Stratford (died 1348) has his monument between the south pillars of the choir, 'near the steps of St. Dunstan's altar' (Parker, 354; 33 in plan). The rich and light canopy work above is sadly mutilated.

Archbishop Bradwardin was buried (at 30) under the new window of St. Anselm's chapel; and his so-called monument consists of some panelling, which lines the wall under the sill of that window.

Archbishop Sudbury has a fine canopied monument next to Stratford (31) 'on the south side of the altar of S. Dunstan,' (Parker, 397); and Archbishop Courtney an altar-tomb (25) at the feet of the Black Prince.

Archbishop Chichely, to use the words of Archbishop Parker, lies 'on the north side of the presbytery (17), in a tomb which he constructed while living' (Parker, p. 427).[f] He was the founder of

---

[e] Engraved in Blore's *Monumental Remains*. All the monuments are engraved in Dart's *History*, and these representations, although wanting in character, are yet most useful in restoring the deficient parts.

[f] Engraved in Skelton's *Pietas Oxoniensis*.

All Souls College, Oxford, and his monument has been put into beautiful order at the expense of that college, and by the skill of Mr. Auſtin, the architect of the cathedral.

Archbishop Kemp's (34) tomb, which is described by Parker (p.437) as ſtanding 'between the archiepiscopal throne and the tomb of John Stratford, at the south door of the presbytery,' is surmounted by a moſt curious double canopy or teſter of wood-work; and it is greatly to be regretted that so valuable a ſpecimen of this class of decoration should be allowed to remain in its present ſtate of dilapidation and neglect.

Archbishop Bourchier has a place of sepulture (19) which was formally granted to him, 'in the ſpace which is in the north part of the choir of our church, between two columns next to the altar of St. Elphege, where now there are closets (armaria) for keeping the things of the altar, And the said monument shall be conſtructed at the expense of the archbishop, of handsome workmanship, and ornamental to the church, but with no superfluous appendages that may sensibly screen the light of the north windows from the altars. Also, in the same ſpace, between the two columns, a new armarium shall be made, in which the things belonging to the altar may be kept as usual. Dated Ap. vi. 1480.'g

The altar of this tomb is remarkable for its resemblance to those of Edward III and Richard II in Weſtminſter abbey, the latter of which is copied from the former. The dates of these altar-tombs are 1377, 1399, and 1480 reſpectively, so that a century intervened between the firſt and laſt.

---

g 'The place of sepulture granted to Thomas Bourchier – In ſpatio quod eſt in Boreali parte chori Ecclesiæ noſtræ inter duas columnas proximas altari S. Elphegi, ubi nunc armaria sunt ad res altaris reponendas: but with this proviso, Quod sumptibus Archiepiscopi dicta sepultura decenti artificio ad honorem Ecclesim conſtruatur, non adeo tamen superfluo ut notabiliter impediat lumen ab ea parte Ecclesiæ a feneſtris Borealibus ad Altaria porrigi, ac etiam quod in eodem ſpacio ac inter duas columnas saltem unum armarium novum ordinetur, in quo res altari pertinentes juxta consuetudinem idonee conservari possunt. Dat. Apr. 16. 1480' (Ex Archivis Ecc. Cant. Battely, App. p. 4).

Of Archbishop Morton, the Obituary says,[h] 'that he was persuaded by some of his friends that he. ought to erect a worthy, ample, and handsome monument for himself, wherefore he chose his burial-place; yet not in public, but in that secret subterraneous retirement termed the crypts, near the image of the Blessed Virgin Mary whom he particularly respected. And there his body lies, covered with marble.' It is a plain altar-tomb, under an arch of the crypt, the sides and soffit of which have been clothed with moldings and tabernacles of the style of his time, of which it furnishes an excellent dated example.

The monument of William Warham, including also a small chantry chapel, is constructed in the north wall of the north transept or martyrdom, and is a very handsome specimen of a very common design.

Lastly, the tomb of Reginald Pole, although beyond the period to which I have limited this enquiry, is yet worth notice, because he was the last Archbishop that was buried in Christ Church. 'Their burials there,' says Somner,[i] 'have been ever since discontinued, a thing, the whilst to some seeming very strange, that of all the archbishops since the Reformation, not one hath chosen to be buried there, but all, as it were, with one consent, declined their own cathedral (the ancient and accustomed place of archiepiscopal sepulture), affecting rather an obscure burial in some one private parish church or other.'

The remarkable remaining monuments of the laity are those of the Black Prince, of Lady Mohun, of Henry IV and his queen, and of Margaret Holland and her two husbands.

h 'Et ubi à nonnullis sæpissimè persuasus erat; ut sibi sepulchrum satis amplum, dignum, honorificumve construeret; non in publico, non in tumultu, sed in secreto subterraneoque loco in criptis nuncupato, lapide duntaxat coopertus marmoreo, coram Imagine Beatissimæ Virginis Mariæ, quam ex intimo diligebat, sepulturæ locum elegit. Ubi ipsius corpus fœlicissimum jam quiescit.' Obit. in Aug. Sac., t. i, p. 64. He founded a chantry here for two priests to say daily mass for his soul. In his will he says, 'Volo et dispono quod corpus meum sepeliatur in Ecclesia mea Cathedrali Cantuar. viz. coram Imagine Beatissimæ Virginis Mariæ, vulgariter nuncupatæ, Our Lady of Undercroft, et quod cooperiatur cum uno plano lapide marmoreo basso absque aliis voluptuosis expensis.' Battely, App. 35.

i Somner, p. 138.

The will of the Black Prince, dated June 7, 1376, about a month before his death (as printed by Nichols, p. 66. *Royal Wills*), contains minute directions for the construction of his tomb, which proves that it was not made in his lifetime.[k] He had previously (in 1363) founded a chantry in the crypt (p. 129). The will of Henry IV, dated Jan. 21, 1408, four years before his death, contains no other direction for his funeral than that 'the body be beryed in the Chirch at Caunterbury aftyr the descrecion of my cousin the Archbyshcopp of Caunterbury (namely Thomas Arundel)... Also y devys and ordeyn that ther be a chauntre perpetuall of twey preestis for to sing and prey for my soul in the aforseyd Chirch of Caunterbury, in soch a plase and aftyr soch ordinaunce as it seemeth best to my aforseyd cousin of Canterbury' (Nichols, *Royal Wills*, p. 203). The monument bears the effigies of the king and of his second queen, Joan of Navarre. Two exquisite engravings of it are in Blore's Monumental Remains, and the same work contains engravings of the monument of Edward the Black Prince.

[k] Nous devisons... n're corps d'estre enseveliz en l' eglise cathedrale, de la Trinite de Canterbire, ou le corps du veray martir mons'r Seint Thomas repose en mylieu de la chapelle de n're dame Undercrofte droitement devant l'autier, siq' le bout de n're tombe devers les pees soit dix peez loinz de l'autier et qe mesme la tombe soit de marbre de bone masonerie faite.' The chapel of our Lady Undercroft is the chapel in the centre of the crypt. But as both the archbishop and the prince were deposited in the Trinity chapel above, in the exact relative positions described, there can be no doubt that some ambiguity or error has crept into the will. 'Et volons qe entour la ditte tombe soient dusze escuchons de laton, chacun de la largesse d'un pie, dont les syx seront de noz armez entiers, et les autres six des plumez d'ostruce, et qe sur chacun escuchon soit escript, c'est assavoir' sur cellez de noz armez et sur les autres des plumes d'ostruce, houmont. Et paramont la tombe soit fait un tablement de laton suzorrez de largesse a longure de meisme la tombe, sur quel nouz voloms q'un ymage d'ov'eigne leve de latoun suzorrez soit mys en memorial de nous, tout armez de fier de guerre de nous armes quartillez et le visage mie, ove notre heaume de leopard mys dessous la teste de l'ymage, et volons qe sur n're tombe en lieu ou leu le purra plus clerement lire et veoir soit escript ce qe ensuit en la maner qe sera mielx aviz a noz executours.' Then follows a long inscription and minute directions for the funeral ceremonies, and a bequest of various jewellery, and especially of drapery to the high altar, to the altar of our Lady in the said chapel (in the crypt), to the altar where 'Monseigneur Saint Thomas' lies (at the head of his shrine, p.127 above), to the altar where his head is kept (in the crypt, see p. 126 above), and to the altar where the point of the sword was (in the Martyrium, p. 45 above).

Lady Mohun of Dunſtar founded a perpetual chantry in 1395, and is buried in the crypt near the altar of the Virgin Mary, under a canopy of clumsy workmanship, which is made to form part of the screen of the lady-chapel. The monument of Margaret Holland and her two husbands has been already mentioned (in p. 141). The following liſt will supply dates and other particulars.

Liſt of the Burial Places of the Archbishops of Canterbury, from Cuthbert to Warham, and of some other personages whose shrines or monuments were placed in the Cathedral

The names of persons whose monuments are ſtill in exiſtence are printed in italics.

Year of death	ARCHBISHOPS	Plan, Fig. 5	BURIAL PLACES
758	Cuthbert	16	At the altar of S. Stephen to the right (pp. 48, 61).
762	Bregwin	38	Behind the altar of S. Gregory to the south (pp. 21, 48, 62).
790	Jambert	—	In the monaſtery of S. Auguſtine.
803	Athelard	15	In the altar of S. Stephen to the left (pp. 48, 61).
829	Vulfred	14	At the altar of S. Martin to the right (pp. 48, 61).
830	Feologild	43	Before the altar of S. Michael to the south (p.43).
870	Chelnoth	8	Behind the altar of S. Benediƈt to the left (p.43).
888	Athelred	—	Close to the south wall of the crypt of Trinity chapel (p. 50).
923	Plegemund	37	Behind the altar of S. Gregory to the north (pp.21, 48, 62).
936	Adhelm	11	Behind the altar of S. Benediƈt to the right (p.43).
941	Vulfelm	7	Before the altar of S. Benediƈt to the left (p.40).
961	Odo	23	Behind the old altar of the Holy Trinity, afterwards removed to the corona (pp. 32, 51, 63, 126).
988	Dunſtan	32	On the south side of the presbytery (pp. 116, 117, 123).
989	Ethelgar	36	At the altar of S. John the Evangeliſt to the right (pp. 51, 62).
994	Siric	—	At the altar of S. Paulinus in the crypt (p.50).
1005	Elfric	35	At the altar of S. John the Evangeliſt to the left (pp. 50, 61).
1012	Elfege	19	On the north side of the presbytery (pp. 116, 126).
1020	Living	12	At the altar of S. Martin to the left (p. 48, 61).
1038	Egelnoth	10	Before the altar of S. benediƈt to the right (p. 43).

1050	Eadsin	—	Close to the north wall of the crypt of Trinity chapel (pp. 50, 51).
1052	Robert	—	Ejected from the see.
1070	Stigand	—	Ejected from the see.
1089	Lanfranc	13	Close to the south wall of Trinity chapel, afterwards removed to the altar of S. Martin (pp. 50, 62).
1109	Anselm	29	Behind the altar of SS. Peter and Paul (p. 50).
1122	Rudolph	6	Chapel of S. Benedict to the left of the entrance (p.43).
1136	William Corboil	9	Chapel of S. Benedict to the right of the entrance (p. 43).
1161	Theobold	3	Close to the north wall of Trinity chapel, afterwards removed to the Lady chapel in the nave (pp. 50, 64).
1170	Thomas à Becket	27	In the crypt; afterwards translated to the great shrine (pp. 51, 69).
1184	Richard	2	In the Lady chapel of the nave (p. 40).
1190	Baldewyn	—	In the Holy Land at Accon. (Gervasii. Act. Pont. Cant. p. 678).
1205	*Hubert Walter*	40	South wall of choir ('in chori pariete ad austrum.' Parker, 233).
1228	*Stephen Langton*	42	In the chapel of S. Michael (Parker, 245).
1231	Richard Wethershed	—	At S. Gemma.
1240	Edmund	—	At Pontiniac.
1270	Boniface	—	In Savoy.
1278	Robert Kilwardby	—	At Viterbo.
1292	*John Peckham*	4	At the north part of the church, near the place of martyrdom of S. Thomas (Regist. Ecc. Cant., *Ang. Sac.*, i, 117).
1313	Robert Winchelsey	39	Near the altar of S. Gregory against the south wall (Parker, 317). 'In a right goodly tumbe of marble at the very but ende yn the waulle side.' Lel. *Itin.*, vol. vi, fol. 3. This was destroyed for his reputed sanctity (Parker, 317).
1327	*Walter Reynolds*	41	South wall of the choir ('in australi chori muro' Parker, 324).
1333	*Simon Mepham*	28	'In quadam capella s^ci Petri nuncupata ex parte australi summi altaris.' Regist. Ecc. Cant., *Ang. Sac.*, 118.
1348	*John Stratford*	33	By the steps of S. Dunstan's altar (Parker, 354).
1349	*Thomas Bradwardin*	30	In the chapel of Anselm at the south wall (Parker, 364).
1366	Simon Islip	1	North side of nave in a marble altar-tomb with a brass, now destroyed (engraved by Dart, 151).
1376	Simon Langham	—	Westminster.
1374	William Wittlesey	46	South side of nave in a marble tomb with a brass, now destroyed (engraved by Dart, 155).
1381	*Simon Sudbury*	31	On the south side of the altar of S. Dunstan (Parker, 397).
1396	*William Courtney*	25	Near the shrine of Thomas à Becket to the south (Parker, 405).

1414	Thomas Arundel	—	In his chapel on the north of the nave (Parker, 413; Somner, 136). 'Under a piller on the north side.' Lel., *It.*, vol. vi, fol. 3. Entirely destroyed, and the exact position unrecorded.
1443	*Henry Chicheley*	17	North side of presbytery in a tomb which he constructed while living (Parker, 427).
1452	John Stafford	—	Martyrium, before the new chapel of the Virgin (Parker, 432).
1454	*John Kemp*	34	Between the archiepiscopal throne and the tomb of John Stratford at the south side of the presytery (Parker, 437).
1486	*Thomas Bourchier*	19	At the north side of the high altar (Parker, 443).
1500	*John Morton*	33	In the crypt, under Archbishop Stratford. 'In a sumptuous chapel constructed by himself' (Parker, 449).
1503	Henry Deane	—	Near the place of Becket's martyrdom (Parker, 453).
1532	*William Warham*	5	In a small chapel which he constructed while living, near the place of Becket's martyrdom (Parker, 488).

RELICS

316	S. Blaise	47	Behind the high altar (pp. 45, 127).
585	S. Salvius	—	Over the high altar (p. 128).
—	S. Vulganius	48	Over the altar of S. Stephen (p. 128).
862	S. Swithin	49	Over the altar of S. Martin (p. 128).
866	S. Audoen	—	In the crypt; afterwards removed to the relic cupboard (pp. 46, 128).
709	S. Wilfred of York	22	Behind the high altar of the Holy Trinity; afterwards removed to the north side of the corona (pp. 50, 62, 126).
—	Siburgis	45	Before the altar of S. Michael to the north (p. 43).

ROYAL AND NOBLE PERSONS

c. 962	Ediva, Queen (of Edw. the Elder?)	12	At the altar of S. Martin under the feretrum of Living (pp. 59, 62).
1376	*Edward the Black Prince*	26	On the south side of Trinity chapel.
c. 1395	*Lady Mohun of Dunstar*	—	In the south screen of the Lady chapel of the crypt.
1410	*John Earl of Somerset*		
1420	*Thomas Duke of Clarence*	44	In S. Michael's chapel. Erected by the widow, in her lifetime.
1440	*Margaret Holland*		
1413	Henry IV	20	In Trinity chapel on the north side. Probably erected by Queen Joan (Sandford, pp. 263, 268).
1437	*Joan of Navarre, his second Queen*		
—	*Isabel Countess of Athol*	28	In the crypt under Archbishop Mepham.

Explanation of the Plan and Section

The Plan (which is referred to throughout as fig. 5) is intended to illustrate the changes that have taken place in the building from the period of Gervase to the present time. Various tints of shading are employed to distinguish the works of different periods. Thus Lanfranc's work is full black; vertical strokes are assigned to Ernulf; diagonal (sloping forward) to William of Sens; horizontal to English William. Subsequent works are dotted, and some uncertain parts are distinguished by a diagonal shading sloping backwards. And in order to compare the plan of the crypt with that of the superstructure, which in this building is necessary, the crypt is introduced into the upper half of the plan in a lighter tint, shaded as for the superstructure, that is, with vertical strokes for Ernulf, and with horizontal for English William. To avoid confusion, the windows are wholly omitted in this upper half of the plan; they are however inserted in the lower half. In this lower half, dates are inserted which refer solely to the vaults. For want of room I have written in many of these cases merely the two last figures of the date, thus, 76 for 1176, but only in that part of the building which belongs to the twelfth century. The other figures of reference apply to monuments and shrines, and ate written respectively as near to the site of each as the size of the plan would allow. As these figures extend only from 1 to 49, there can be no ambiguity between them and the date figures, which are all greater than 75. Letters of reference are reserved for the other purposes of the plan, and Roman numerals are applied to distinguish the piers. An accidental coincidence between pier x, and the site of the high Altar marked X, might have led to confusion, but with this notice they can easily be distinguished from each other. To have introduced the vault-ribs throughout this plan would have made it too intricate; a few only are inserted here and there, where particular explanations required them. Thus in the lower half of the plan the compartments or 'ciboria' of the choir and side-aisles are separated by a line which marks the transverse rib of the vault, but in the side-aisle of the presbytery

I have found it necessary to lay down also the other ribs, which present a singular irregularity (see p. 101). One compartment of the nave and its side. aisle vault are inserted, also one compartment of the Lady chapel, and one of St. Michael's chapel.

The Section, fig. 6, which stands immediately over the Plan, and is drawn to the same scale, is a mere diagram, drawn in block as it is called, in which all the parts introduced are of the proper magnitude, and the pier-arches of the proper form, but all lesser portions are omitted, even to the arches of the triforium, and the windows of the clerestory. Its principal object is to note the progress of the work as described by Gervase. The figures upon it all indicate dates, and the two first figures are omitted in most of those that belong to the twelfth century. Each pier has its date, but in the upper works the date figure is placed at the beginning and end of each year's work; thus 78 . . . . . 78, 84 . . . . . 84, shews the extent of the works of 1178 and 1184 respectively, and the place where they join. The full average date is written upon the nave and tower works, and upon the buttressing arches. It was thought unnecessary to extend the plan to the whole length of the nave.

A List of the Dated Examples of Architectural Works in Canterbury Cathedral

1. Nave, choir, crypt, transepts, and western towers of Lanfranc, the only remains of which are a few patches of masonry. The north-western tower taken down in 1834 is preserved by drawings. — 1070 to 1077

2. Enlarged choir, eastern transepts, crypt and chapels of St. Andrew, St. Anselm, and Trinity, the works of Anselm, Ernulf, and Conrad, of which there remain the crypt, the external walls of the other portions, and the chapels of St. Anselm and St. Andrew. — c. 1096 to c. 1110

3. Present choir, by William of Sens.   1175 to 1178
4. Trinity chapel, its crypt and corona.   1179 to 1184
5. Monument, in the martyrdom, of Archbishop
    Peckham, who died in   1292
6. Choir wall of enclosure, &c.
    by Prior Henry de Estria.   1304 and 1305
7. Screen and monument in Anselm's chapel,
    of Archbishop Mepham, who died in   1333
8. Window of Anselm's chapel by prior Henry de Estria   1336
9. Monument of Archbishop Stratford, who died in   1348
10. Remains of Archbishop Bradwardin's monument
    in Anselm's chapel, he died in   1349
11. Chantry of the Black Prince in the south
    transept of the crypt, soon after   1363
12. Monument of the Black Prince, who died in   1376
13. Nave, western transepts, and chapel of St.
    Michael, by Prior Chillenden   (to c.1410) c.1378
14. Monument of Archbishop Sudbury, who died in   1381
15. Monument of Lady Mohun of Dunstar in the crypt   c. 1395
16. Monument of Archbishop Courtney, who died in   1396
17. Chantry chapel and monument of Henry IV,
    who died in   1412
18. Monument of Margaret Holland and
    her two husbands   c. 1420 to c. 1437
19. Monument of Archbishop Chichely erected
    by himself, he died in   1443
20. The New Lady chapel and the south-west
    campanile by Prior Goldston I, who held that
    office from   1449 to 1468
21. Monument of Archbishop Kemp, who died in   1454
22. Monument of Cardinal Bourchier, erected
    between   1480 and 1486
23. The central tower and buttressing arches,
    by Prior Goldston II   c. 1495

24. Monument of Cardinal Morton, erected by
    himself, he died in   1500
25. Monument of Archbishop Warham, erected by
    himself, he died in   1532

List of the Principal Works and Editions Referred to

Anglia Sacra, 1691.

Historiæ Anglicanæ Scriptores X, 1652, contains the following works of Gervase, Chronica Gervasii :

Tractatus de combustione et reparatione Doroborniensis Ecclesiæ.

Chronica de tempore Regum Angliæ, Stephani, Hen. II. and Ric. I. Actus Pontificum Cantuariensis Ecclesiæ.

Edmeri Opuscula. I have employed the MS. which is preserved in the library of Corpus Christi College, Cambridge, but I have also referred to the printed copies of those parts which I have employed, and which have been published as follows:

Vita S. Wilfridi. Mabillon *Sæc. Benedict*. iii. p. 196. He omits some pages at the end (p. 17 above).

Vita S. Odonis. Mabillon *Sæc. Benedict*. v. p. 283. Ang. Sac., t. ii. p. 78.

Vita S. Dunstani, with some omissions in Ang. Sac., t. ii. p. 211.

Liber de Miraculis S. Dunstani. Mabillon has published a fragment of this, t. vii. p. 709. (See pages 14 and 16 above.)

Vita S. Bregwini. *Ang. Sac.*, t. ii. p. 184.

Epistola de Corpore S. Dunstani, &c. *Ang. Sac.*, p. 222.

De reliquiis S. Audoeni. (This has never been published entire. See pp. 5, 10 above.)

Edmeri Historia Novorum, Lond. 1623.

Matth. Parkeri Cant^s. Arch^i., *de Antiquitate Britannicæ Ecclesiæ*, Lond. 1729.

In Wilkins' *Concilia* are the following articles relating to the Architectural History of Canterbury Cathedral:

Constitutiones Lanfranci, vol. i. p. 328.

Vol. ii. p. 244. Statuta domiui R. de Winchelsey archiepiscopi in prima visitatione sua in capitulo Cantuar. Ex MS. Cott. Galba, E. 4.

Mandatum archiepiscopi Cant. de charitativa subventione pro fabrica ecclesiæ. Ex reg. Sudbury, fol. 52, a, (vol. iii. p. 136).

Process against Thomas Becket, and order for demolishing his shrine at Canterbury, (vol. iii. p. 835).

The king's letter for taking away shrines and images. Ex reg. Cranmer. fol. 18, a, (vol. iii. p. 857).

D. Erasmi Roterod., *Colloquia*, 1524. The 'peregrinatio religionis ergo' contains a very curious visit to the relics of Canterbury, which has been quoted by all writers on this subject.

The principal works that especially relate to the Cathedral are as follows :

The Antiquities of Canterbury, by William Somner, first published in 1640. I have referred to the second edition by Nicholas Battely, 1703, to which was added, as a second part,

Cantuaria Sacra, by Nic. Battely, 1703.

A Walk in and about the City of Canterbury, by W. Gostling. 2 Ed. 1777.

The History and Antiquities of the Cathedral Church of Canterbury, by the Rev. J. Dart, 1727.

Twelve Perspective Views of... the Metropolitical Church of Canterbury, &c., by Charles Wild, 1807.

A Graphical Illustration of... the Cathedral Church of Canterbury, by W. Woolnoth, 1816.

History and Antiquities of the Metropolitical Church of Canterbury, by J. Britton, 1821.

Winkle's *Architectural and Picturesque Illustration of the Cathedral Churches*, Canterbury, in vol. i.

Storer's *Cathedral Churches*, 1814.

The Archæologia contains several papers on this subject, by Mr. Ledwich, Mr. Denne, and Mr. Saunders. See vol. viii. p. 174; vol. x. p. 37; vol. xi. 375; and vol. xvii. p. 17.

Carter's *Ancient Architecture and Sculpture* has several engravings.

I have also had occasion to quote the two following tracts of my own, viz.:

'On the Construction of the Vaults of the Middle Ages', *Transactions of the Royal Institute of British Architects*, vol. i. pt. 2, 1842.

Architectural Nomenclature of the Middle Ages, No. IX. of the publications of the Cambridge Antiquarian Society. Cambridge, 1844.

Additional Notes, and Corrections

[Where possible, these have been incorporated into the text.
Only those which have not are printed here.]

p. 28, l. 3. It may be necessary to add that the present crypt and confessionary of St. Peter's are totally different in plan and extent from the ancient one, and apparently on a higher level.

p. 40, note *j*. The position of the Lady chapel was similarly confirmed in 1787, when 'the workmen began to take up the old pavement in the body of Canterbury cathedral, and in levelling the ground for the new pavement at the east end of the north aisle, a leaden coffin was found a little below the surface, containing the remains of a body that had been wrapped in a robe of velvet or rich silk fringed with gold; these remains were much decayed. In the coffin was likewise enclosed an inscription on a plate of lead in capital letters, engraved in double strokes with a sharp-pointed instrument.' *Archæol.*, vol. xv. p. 294. An engraving of the inscription is added, and shews that the personage so interred was Archbishop Theobald; it runs thus, 'Hic requiescit venerabilis memorie Theobaldus Cantuarie archiepiscopus Britanie' &c.: and as Gervase relates (p. 62) that this archbishop was buried in a leaden coffin before the altar of St. Mary in the nave, this discovery at once confirms his accuracy, and assists us in determining the exact position of the altar in question.

p. 44. A stone is still pointed out on the pavement in front of *P*, which tradition assigns as the exact spot on which Becket fell; a small piece has been cut out of it, which is said to be still preserved at Rome. In some of the monastic representations of Becket's fall he is slain at the very foot of an altar, but this is only introduced to heighten the sacrilege. The altar at *P* was erected afterwards, and the nearest altar was that of St. Benedict at *M*. Thus comparing representations of this murder on the seats of the archbishops, that of Boniface 1259 has no altar; on the seal of Robert 1273 the altar is in the background, and Becket has his back to it; on the seal of John Peckham 1278 the altar again disappears, but in the seal of John Stratford the victim kneels at the altar with his back to his assailants, and this position is retained in the seals of Islip, Langham, and Arundel.

p. 47, l. 15. See note *s*, p. 122.

p. 50, l. 1. SS. Bregwin and Plegemund were removed hither and placed behind this altar, in consequence of the attempt of the monk Lambert to carry off the relics of St. Bregwin (see p. 18). Osbern says the bodies were placed in two 'scrinia,' 'supra altare.' The figures of reference in the plans are for want of room before the altar instead of behind it, as they ought to be.

p. 50, l. 9. The tower of St. Anselm, and the opposite one of St. Andrew, are at present only of the same height as the clerestory of the Norman church, to which they formed appendages, and consequently they rose above the side-aisles of that church as much as the clerestory did. The external faces of the inward walls of these towers are now enclosed under the roof of William's triforium, and it may be seen that they were once exposed to the weather. It is difficult to understand why they were termed lofty, or even towers, unless we suppose that they once rose much higher. The small staircase-turrets on the western sides of the transepts deserve the epithets much better.

p. 62, note *q*. The corona may also mean the aisle which often circumscribes the east end of an apsidal church, and which with its radiating chapels may be said to crown its eastern extremity.

p. 64, l. 10. See note above to p. 40.

p. 54. From the account which follows it may be gathered that the two sides of the work, the north and south, were carried on symmetrically, exactly as much being always done on one side as on the other.

p. 69. Archbishop Sudbury, in the preamble to his indulgence for rebuilding the nave, describes the church as dedicated to the Holy Trinity by the blood of the martyr Thomas. 'Quam digne, quamque meritorie landandus est locus ille celeberrimus ecclesiæ nostræ, viz. Cant. metropolitica, omnium ecclesiarum regni Angliæ caput, et præcipua, ad ipsius veri Dei, æterni, incomprehensibilis, omnipotentis trinitatis, Patris scil. Filii et Spiritus Sancti gloriam et honorem constructus, et sanguine sanctissimi Thomæ martyris, dudum Cantuar. archiepiscopi patroni nostri in eo nuper martyrizati, dedicatus' (Wilkins' *Concilia,* vol. iii. p. 136).

p. 73. In the plan of Lanfranc's nave, fig. 3, I have represented it as having three western doors in imitation of its original at Caen, but I have no other authority for so doing. The present entrance is by a porch on the south side of the southern campanile at X.

p. 83, l. 8. That these pillars are wholly the work of William is shewn by their solid masonry (described in note *l*, p. 86), and their bases, and also by the fact recorded by Gervase, that the weakening of the old pillars by the fire was the cause that compelled the entire destruction of these' pillars and all that they supported.'

p. 90, l. 14. The fact of the pillar in fig. 23 being placed immediately under the pier X in the choir above, was verified by measurements taken for that express purpose.

p. 104, l. 30. This mode of constructing the triforium arches was tried and abandoned in the subsequent work by the Frenchman, on the south side of the choir between the pillars V, VI, fig. 5. The view of the opposite triforium through the arches in fig. 7, p. 63, shews these two kinds of triforial arcades.

p. 107. l. 26. The mechanical construction of the triforium and clerestory and the opening here mentioned, is shewn in fig. 7, p. 63.

p. 117, note *b*. Somner, p. 99, is the authority whence Dart copied the bequest of £20 by John Bokingham to the high Altar.

Index

A

Adelais, Queen 20
Adhelm, Archbishop 44
Ælfheah. *See* Elfege
Alan, Prior
  transfers bodies of Dunstan and
    Elfege at night 59
Alfwin 17
All Saints, altar of 43
All Souls College, Oxford 147
Alphege. *See* Elfege
altar of St. Audoen 50
altar of St. Augustine 50
altar of St. Gregory 49
altar of St. John Baptist 50
altar of St. John the Evangelist 50
altar of St. Katherine 50
altar of St. Martin 61
altar of the Virgin Mary 126
altars, list of 42
ambo 28
Andrew, St.
  altar of 49
  chapel of 127
  tower of 67
Angel Steeple 40, 142–144, 143
Anglia Sacra 1, 2, 7
Ann, St.
  chapel of 141
Annals of Rochester Cathedral 19
Anselm, Archbishop 18, 21, 46, 71,
    81
  altar of 50
  chapel of 146
  chapel window 130–132

Anselm, St.
  tower of 67
apse 42, 43, 44, 48
apse of St. Michael 49
apse of St. Stephen 49
Arundel, Thomas, Archbishop 133,
    137, 149
  gives bells 134
'Arundel ryng' 134
Arundell. *See* Arundel
Athelard, Archbishop
  remains deposited at altar of St.
    Stephen 61
  tomb of 48
Audoen, St. 5
  altar of 50
  relics of 5, 6, 7
Augustine, St., Abbey of
  Jambert buried in 43
Augustine, St., of Canterbury 1, 23,
    28, 48
  altar of 50
aula 12, 30, 31, 40
Austin, George 147
Austroberta, St.
  head of 13

B

Baldwin, Archbishop
  appointment of 68
baptistery 33
Beaufort, Edmund, Duke of Somer-
    set, Count of Mortain 141
Beaufort, John, Earl of Somerset 141
Bec, abbey of 18

Becket's Crown
  origin of name 63
Becket, Thomas à. *See* Thomas, St.,
  Becket
Bede, Venerable
  *Ecclesiastical History of the English
  People* 1, 10
Benedict, St.
  altar of 43
Benedictine order 79
Benoit, St., church of, at Paris 32
Bernini, Gianlorenzo 27
Black Prince 129, 146, 148, 149
Blaise, St. 3
  altar of 43
  burial place 45
  tomb of 120
Blasius, St.. *See* Blaise, St.
Bourchier, Thomas, Archbishop 147
Boys, Sir John 42
Bradwardin, Archbishop 146
Bregwin, Archbishop 3, 50
  tomb of 14
Bregwyn, St.
  monks guard relics of 20
Britton, John 42
Brixworth, Saxon church at 29, 33
Bromton. *See* Brompton, John
Brompton, John 20
Burgh. *See* Peterborough
Burrough, Sir James 120

C
Caen 39
  abbey church of the Holy Trinity
  77, 85
  Abbey of St. Etienne 42, 72
    similarities with Christ Church
    72
  Lanfranc abbot of 14
Calixtus, Pope
  prefers Thurstan and Hugo over
    Radulf 44

Canterbury
  Roman church at 1, 10, 23
  sacked by Danes 59
  Saxon cathedral at 23–34
Canterbury, archbishops of
  burial places of 43
Canute. *See* Cnut
Cerisy, abbey at 42
chancel
  completed by Conrad 19
chantry chapel 141, 148
Chartham, William 136
Chelnoth, Archbishop
  burial place of 44
Chichely, Hhenry, Archbishop 146
Chichester Cathedral 79
Chillenden, Thomas, Prior 124, 135,
  138, 142
  ornaments high altar 117
choir 43
  transverse section of 82
choir, 'glorious' 35, 36, 84
choir of monks 78
choir of singers 29, 31, 78
chorus. *See* choir of singers
Christ Church Cathedral
  history of the name 20
  plan of 41
  ciborium 54
civery. *See* severy
Clarence, Thomas Lancaster, Duke
  of 141
clavis 54
Clemente, St., church of 28, 31
Cnut, King 8, 9
confessio. See confessionary
confessionary 12, 26
Conrad, Prior 71
  and 'glorious' choir 35, 45–51, 84,
    116, 121, 122
  completes Ernulf's chancel 19
Constantine, Emperor 28
corona 40, 48

Corpus Christi College, Cambridge
10
Cotman, John Sell
Normandy 42
Courtenay, William, Archbishop
134, 137, 146
Courtney. *See* Courtenay
Cranmer, Thomas, Archbishop
complains that King's orders are
ignored 114
Cromwell, Thomas, Earl of Essex
commands destruction od St.
Thomas's bones 113
crypt 43, 48, 128–130
unfinished columns of 76, 78
crypt, western
survives fire of 1174 81
work of Ernulf 83
Culmer, Richard 118
Cathedral News 119
Cuthbert, Archbishop 2, 3
erects baptistery 33
in Rome 2
obtains right to bury within cathedral 2, 48
remains deposited at altar of St.
Stephen 62
tomb of 14, 48

D

Dado. *See* Audoen
Danes
sack Canterbury in 101 7, 59
David, King of Scots 20, 21
Diceto, Ralph de 20
Dover
church of St. Martin 44
Dunstan, Archbishop 6
coffin moved to refectory 16
remains moved 37–38
saves refectory and dormitory
from fire 13
tomb of 6–7, 12, 29, 31, 58

Dunstan, Archbishop
relics of 114
Dunstan, St.
altar of 47, 116, 117, 146
image of 48
Durham Cathedral 125
nave 126
tabernacle-work 117

E

Eadbrith, King of Kent 2
Eadmer. *See* Edmer the singer
Eadsin, Archbishop
tomb of 50
Eadwine the scribe
drawing of Christ Church 50
east end
Saxon cathedral's entrance at 24
Eastry, Kent 109
Edgar, King 5
Ediva, Queen
burial place of 43, 59
remains deposited at altar of St.
Martin 62
Edmer the singer 1, 16, 24, 29, 33, 39,
40, 45, 80
History of Recent Events 8, 14–15,
19
Letter on the Body of St. Dunstan
7, 9
Life of Odo 3, 6
Life of St. Audoen 5, 6
Life of St. Bregwin 2, 3, 9, 14, 17
Life of St. Dunstan 7
Life of St. Oswald 3
Life of St. Wilfrid 4, 15, 17, 31
Miracles of St. Dunstan 14, 15
On the Relics of St. Audoen 7, 10
Edward III 147
Edward of Woodstock, Prince of
Wales (the Black Prince) 129
Edward the Confessor
chapel, Westminster 113

Edwyn the scribe. *See* Eadwine the scribe
Egelnoth, Archbishop 8, 9
  burial place of 44
Elfege, Archbishop 7, 32, 147
  altar of 47, 116, 117
  body moved to refectory 16
  body returned to Canterbury 8
  captured by Danes 39
  coffin moved to choir 38
  deposits head of St. Swithin 11
  image of 48
  relics of 114
  tomb of 58
Elphege. *See* Elfege
Ely Cathedral 42, 79
  nave of 87
Erasmus of Rotterdam 124, 126
Erkenwald, St.
  altar of 129
Ernulf, Prior 18, 71, 80
  crypt 91
  distinguishing work from that of William of Sens 85–100
  leaves chancel unfinished 19
  made bishop of Rochester 18
  made prior 18
  nationality 18
  rebuilds Peterborough Cathedral 19
  work in crypt of western choir 83
Estria, Henry de. *See* Henry de Estria
Ethelred, Archbishop
  tomb of 50

F
faldistoria 120
Feologild, Archbishop
  burial place of 43
fire of 1011 9–10, 14
fire of 1174 35
free sepulture

Cuthbert obtains right of 2, 48
Fursey, St.
  head of 12

G
Gervase 81, 133
  account of Thomas Becket's martyrdom 44
  Acts of the Archbishops of Canterbury 2, 3, 8, 15, 40
  Tract on the fire and restoration of the church of Canterbury 8, 10, 35–59
Gibbons, Grinling 121
Glastonbury Abbey
  asserts right to Dunstan's remains 59
'glorious' choir 35, 45, 116, 121, 122
Gloucester Cathedral 79
  north transept 141
Godmersham, Kent
  parsonage appropriated 133
Goldston, Thomas, Prior 59, 140, 142, 143, 144
great altar 47, 48, 49, 61
Gregory I, Pope
  altar dedicated to 12, 49
  altar of 21
Gregory III, Pope 2, 28

H
Henry De Estria, Prior 45, 109, 123, 130
  stone tracery 121
Henry I, King of England 19, 21
Henry IV, King of England 141, 148, 149
Hereford Cathedral 79
  Lady Chapel at 79
high altar 60, 116
Holland, Margaret 141, 148, 150
Hollar, Wenceslaus
  plan of Christ Church 115, 122, 127

Holy Trinity
  altar of
    broken up 62
  chapel of 50, 57
  Christ Church dedicated as 20
Holy Trinity chapel 67
Hugo, abbot of St. Augustine 44

I

infirmary
  destroyed by fire 37
Innocent III, Pope 27
Innocents, altar of the 49

J

Jambert, Archbishop 2
Joan of Navarre 149
John the Apostle, St.
  altar of
    built from materials of Holy
      Trinity chapel 62
John the Baptist, St.,
  altar of 50
  church dedicated to 2, 3
    burnt down 1011 10

K

Katherine, St.
  altar of 50
Kemp, John, Archbishop 147

L

Lady Chapel 16, 32, 121, 124, 126, 140
  Archbishop Richard buried in 40
Lambert
  tries to take body of St. Bregwin
    20
Lancaster, Thomas, Duke of
    Clarence 141
lancet windows 106
Lanfranc, Archbishop 14–18, 18, 21,
    23, 39, 45, 46, 133
  church of 71–80

cross of 48, 49
death of 15
his choir pulled down 45
remains badly decomposed 64
remains placed at altar of St.
    Martin 64
remains placed temporarily in
    vestiarium 63
similarity between his Christ
    Church and St. Etienne,
    Caen 72–77
Statutes 60, 79
tomb of 50
Langton, Stephen, Archbishop 141,
    146
Lateran, St. John in, basilica of 28
Laud, Archbishop 118
Leland, John 141
Leo III, Pope 28
Liberius, Pope 28
lierne vault 129
Living, Archbishop
  remains deposited at altar of St
    Martin 61
  tomb of 48, 62
Lorenzo, St., basilica of 27, 28, 32
Lorenzo fuori le mure, church of 28

M

majestatem Domini 48
Maria in Cosmedin, St., church of
    28
Maria Maggiore, St., church of 28
Martin, St. 12
  altar of 48, 61, 62
Martin, St., church of at Dover 44
martyrium of St. Thomas Becket 48
Mary, B. V. 13
Mary, Blessed Virgin
  chapel of 140
    destroyed by fire 37
Mary, blessed virgin
  altar of 48

Mary II, Queen 121
Mary Magdalene, St.
  altar of 48
    Matthew Paris 20, 136
Mepham, Archbishop
  monumental screen 96
Mepham, Simon, Archbishop 146
Michael, St.
  apse of 49
  chapel of 121, 140, 146
Michael, St., altar of 43
Michael of Thydenhanger 136
Mohun of Dunstar, Lady 148
Molasch, William 142
Monasticon 79
monuments 145–153
Morton, John, Archbishop 143, 148
mosaic pavement 113

N

nave 40, 133
  pulled down by Simon Sudbury
    137
Nevers Cathedral 32
Neville Chapel 125
Nicholas, St.
  altar of 48
Nicodemus, gospel of
  attached to pillar 126
Nixon, Dorothy 123
north tower 12
Norwich Cathedral 79

O

Odo, Archbishop 3, 4, 5, 23, 28, 40
  adds clerestory 33
  coffin moved from Holy Trinity
    chapel to choir 62
  death of 5
  deposits Wilfrid's relics in the
    great altar 31
  raises walls 33
  tomb of 6, 32, 50

translates body of St. Wilfrid 11
opus Alexandrinum 113
oratory of the Blessed Virgin Mary
  13
Osbern 2, 13
  life of St. Dunstan 7, 14
Osbert. *See* Edmer the singer
Ouen. *See* Audoen

P

Parker, Matthew, Archbishop 116,
  145, 146
Paschal I, Pope 28
patriarchal chair 115
Peckham, Surrey 19
Peckham, John, Archbishop 146
Percy, Henry, Earl of Northumber-
  land 141
perpendicular style 143
Peter, St., at Rome
  plan of ancient basilica 24
  Saxon Christ Church's resem-
    blance to 24, 29, 33
Peter and Paul, Church of Apostles
  2
Peterborough
  Ernulf made abbot of 18
Peterborough Cathedral 79
  Ernulf rebuilds 19
  tabernacle-work 117
pier-arches
  number in choir at Canterbury
    and elsewhere 74–75
Plegemund, Archbishop 3
  relics removed to south part of
    cathedral 20
  tomb of 50
Pole, Reginald, Archbishop 148
polyandrum 25
portic 42
porticus 42
Prassede, St., church of 27
presbytery 24, 29, 58

Prynne, William 118
puritan depredations 119

R

Radulf, Archbishop 20
  burial place of 44
  passed over by Calixtus 44
Ralph de Diceto 20
reliquary chests 37
Reynolds, Walter, Archbishop 146
Richard, Archbishop 40, 60
  buried in Lady Chapel 40
Richard II 147
Ripon, monastery of 4
Robert, Duke of Normandy 19
Rochester Cathedral 73, 79
  Ernulf erects new buildings 19
Roman church in Canterbury 23

S

St-George de Boscherville, abbey
      at 42
St. Alban's Cathedral
  tabernacle work 117
St. Augustine's Abbey 2
Saxon cathedral 23–34
  plan of 30
scrinium 16
Seez, cathedral at 42
Selden, John 12
Sellyng, William, Prior 142, 143
severy 55
Siburgis,
  remains of 43
Simon of Sudbury. *See* Sudbury,
      Simon, Archbishop
south aisle
  arches in illustrated 65
south door 11–12
south tower 12
St.Alban's Cathedral 79
St. Lucian, monastery of, Beauvais
      18

stalls 120
Stephen, St.
  abbey of, Caen. *See* Caen, abbey of
      St. Etienne
  altar of 48, 61
  apse of 49
Stowe, John
  description of shrine of St. Tho-
      mas Becket 113
Stratford, John, Archbishop 146, 147
Sudbury, Simon, Archbishop 133,
      146
  pulls down nave 137
Swithin, St.
  head deposited by Elfege 11
Sylvester, Pope 28

T

tabernacle-work 116–117
Tenison, Archbishop
  throne 121
Theodbold, Archbishop 145.
      See Theobold, Archbishop
  body translated to Lady Chapel 42
  buried before altar of St. Mary 64
  remains well-preserved 63–64
Thomas, St., Becket 50
  bones destroyed by command of
      Thomas Cromwell 113
  chapel of 67, 113
    work of English William 102
  chapel wall begun 62
  eastern end of cathedral enlarged
      to accomodate chapel of 57
  martyrium of 48, 61, 143
  pallium and *sudarium* 127
  place or martyrdom 44, 51
  shrine described by Stowe 113
  skull 126
  statues of his murderers 126
Thurstan, Archbishop of York 44
tower, central 136, 142–144
tower, great 40

tower, south-west 140
tower of St. Andrew 49, 96
towers of St. Anselm and St. Andrew 67
trellasdome 126
triforium 55, 85
  meanings of 46
triforium of choir
  illustration of 63
Trinity Chapel 141, 145
  plan of the crypt 41
  new, built by English William 102

V

Vatican archives 24
vestiarium 63
Vigilius, Pope 28
Vulfelm, Archbishop
  burial place of 44
Vulfred, Archbishop
  tomb of 48

W

Walter, Hubert, Archbishop 146
Warham, William, Archbishop 59, 148
Westminster Abbey
  tabernacle-work 117
Westminster abbey 113, 147
Westwell, Kent
  parsonage appropriated 133
Wharton, Henry 136
Wilfrid, St., Archbishop of York 4
  body of 31
  coffin moved from Holy Trinity chapel to choir 62
  festival of 17

relics of 4, 6, 11, 16, 18, 80
remains deposited at altar of St. Martin 61
tomb of 50
William, Archbishop 21
  burial place of 43
William, English 54, 81
  and Trinity Chapel side-aisles 106
  distinguishing work from that of William of Sens 102
  takes over building work 57
William of Malmesbury 8, 18
William of Sens 38, 54, 81
  distinguishing work from that of English William 102
  distinguishing work from that of Ernulf 85–100
  his chiselled ornament compared with earlier axe-cut mouldings 65
  injured in fall, 1178 56
  pillars 12 ft higher than Ernulf's 83
  responsible for pillars of choir 83
William of Worcester 55
Willis, Browne
  surveys of cathedrals 79
Winchelsey, Archbishop
  enthronement 120
  statutes of 113
  tomb destroyed 115
Winchester Cathedral 79, 139
  tabernancle-work 117
Winchester Cthedral 42
Winkles, Benjamin and Henry 42
Wodnesbergh, John 142
Worcester Cathedral 79

TIGER OF THE STRIPE

Typeset in the United Kingdom by
TIGER OF THE STRIPE
in Adobe OpenType Minion Pro,
designed by Robert Slimbach, and
Hoefler & Freer-Jones English Textura,
based on a fount cut by
Henric Pieterszoon Lettersnijder
in around 1492.
Old English set in Edlund Insular
designed by
Carl Edlund Anderson.

M M V I

Lightning Source UK Ltd.
Milton Keynes UK
UKOW04f1143151113

221148UK00001B/17/A